Kabbalah

Understanding and Applying
Kabbalistic History Concepts

*(Secret Knowledge Tree of Life Jewish Mysticism
Qabalah Magick and the Spiritual Life)*

Michael Dunphy

Published By **Andrew Zen**

Michael Dunphy

All Rights Reserved

Kabbalah: Understanding and Applying Kabbalistic History Concepts (Secret Knowledge Tree of Life Jewish Mysticism Qabalah Magick and the Spiritual Life)

ISBN   978-1-77485-948-3

No part of this guidebook shall be reproduced in any form without permission in writing from the publisher except in the case of brief quotations embodied in critical articles or reviews.

Legal & Disclaimer

The information contained in this ebook is not designed to replace or take the place of any form of medicine or professional medical advice. The information in this ebook has been provided for educational & entertainment purposes only.

The information contained in this book has been compiled from sources deemed reliable, and it is accurate to the best of the Author's knowledge; however, the Author cannot guarantee its accuracy and validity and cannot be held liable for any errors or omissions. Changes are periodically made to this book. You must consult your doctor or get professional medical advice before using any of the suggested remedies, techniques, or information in this book.

Upon using the information contained in this book, you agree to hold harmless the Author from and against any damages, costs, and expenses, including any legal fees potentially resulting from the application of any of the information provided by this guide. This disclaimer applies to any damages or injury caused by the use and application, whether directly or indirectly, of any advice or information presented, whether for breach of contract, tort, negligence, personal injury, criminal intent, or under any other cause of action.

You agree to accept all risks of using the information presented inside this book. You need to consult a professional medical practitioner in order to ensure you are both able and healthy enough to participate in this program.

TABLE OF CONTENTS

Introduction 1

Chapter 1: What Exactly Is Kaballah 8

Chapter 2: Core Kabbalah Concepts 35

Chapter 3: The Sefer Yetzirah 72

Chapter 4: The Zohar 90

Chapter 5: Kabbalah As A Spiritual Practice 124

Chapter 6: All You Need To Learn About The History Of Fortune Telling 132

Chapter 7: Discover The Major Arcana. 144

Chapter 8: Kabbalah Basics 159

Introduction

Kabbalah is a system of belief which believes that spirituality is the primary reason behind everything. It is traced back to early Jewish sacred texts like the Zohar and various other works composed in Aramaic. It reveals God's creative power throughout all things, and teaches us that we can harness that power to perform miracles since we are one of many extensions of God. This article provides a comprehensive background of Kabbalah and will help you understand how you can apply it to your life.

The term Kabbalah originates in Kabbalah, which is the Hebrew word Qabbala meaning "wisdom." The first known usage of the word comes in the 12th century Kabbalistic texts. Zohar is a term used in Kabbalistic texts from the 12th century. Zohar refers to refer to the specific kind of Jewish mysticism that emphasizes the need to discover ways to get rid of materialistic thinking and to be in harmony with the forces of good and evil.

The foundations of Kabbalah was laid out in an ancient text referred to as"the Torah (Lyra). It begins with the phrases: "In the beginning, God created Heaven and Earth." The text focuses on four distinct people that represent a different part in God's work. One of them is lowest form of the earth's dust and refers to Adam and the descendants of Adam. The second man is created by breathing of God and represents the living creatures. The third man is a shadow made by God's body. It symbolizes evil. Finally, there's an angel named Metatron who is suspended in the air. The angel guides people to understanding and wisdom.

This quote illustrates some the fundamental concepts of Kabbalah:

Kabbalah affirms that human beings aren't just physical beings but also possess an element of spirituality. When we die the physical body goes to sleep while our spiritual body continues to live.

Kabbalah believes that all things that exists in this universe composed of God's forces. This includes animals and humans and other religions have spirits and souls that are distinct from the body, however Kabbalah does not believe in this. Kabbalah is a way of showing how everything is interconnected , and that we are all part of God regardless of what shape we adopt.

Kabbalah is a teaching that when people suffer and suffering, they are not capable of receiving the full portion of God's strength within the person. The people who are suffering should make time to pray for direction from God. Through the power of God believers can perform miracles. God's power isn't limited to the physical realm, but can be felt through the hearts and minds.

Kabbalah believes that one is one of the extensions from God (they are immortalized from God) Therefore, they are eternal.

The beliefs of Kabbalah are similar to those of other religions, however Kabbalah is the only one that fully encompasses these beliefs. Many religions claim that humans are just physical creatures that God made, but Kabbalah shows us the ways we got here from a different source. It also shows us how could be done to enhance our life by exercising our free will.

The Kabbalah belief system was founded on the notion the idea that God is the originator of all clothing, and that we are able to tap into that source by utilizing a method known by the name of "the Kabbalah." The term "Kabbalah" refers to "tradition," and it is a set of beliefs, doctrines and practices that comprise the foundation part of Kabbalah. Kabbalah system. It is vital to understand that the Kabbalah rituals can trace their roots to earlier texts like the Zohar.

Many scholars of religion think they believe that the Kabbalah was conceived through Moses de Leon, who lived in Spain in the 1160s A.D. This theory has been challenged by some historians because there is no evidence to prove Moses de Leon's existence , or anything else regarding his life or work. But, if we take his principles as a basis to understand the nature of what

Kabbalah is and is today, we can understand how it has changed throughout the years.

The term "Kabbalah" is a reference to "tradition." The particular tradition is a reference to the practices and beliefs related to Judaism. These beliefs were handed down through generations, until eventually they were put together into a collection of written work. Kabbalah Kabbalah is a collection of teachings that came into be referred to as"the "received Tradition" in the latter part of the Middle Ages, and it was recorded in the books of the 16th century and onwards.

As well as being a sacred book beliefs, Kabbalah also contains practices which are intended to improve the spirituality of a person and improve their well-being. One of them is using an Hebrew alphabet to form mysterious symbols, referred to as "Qliphoth." This is also known by the name of "Kabbalistic writing" that is the use of Hebrew letters to create the names of negative forces in your mind. The idea behind this technique is that by calling out these harmful entities, you can induce them to withdraw and not cause harm to you, while aiding in improving your spiritual health.

The method works this way It is that you first make an inventory of all names and symbols that you are familiar with and then go through each one by one at a time, and record it alongside its symbol. After you've completed the process for every name you have listed The next step is to examine all the individual symbols in order and attempt to make connections between the symbols. This is quite complicated because there are many different combinations of symbols could be made from the same letters. It is nevertheless crucial to attempt to comprehend the symbols and make connections between them.

Once you've completed the process, you will need to reverse the process and examine each symbol in turn. The intention is that, through this, you'll be in a position to "un-see" any negative forces which were previously evident within your head. You can then utilize the positive forces to create power in your own life.

The Kabbalah includes rituals that are designed to boost your health and enable you to lead a healthier lifestyle. One of these rituals is called"the "Prayer of the 8 Gates" which demands that you consume just eight specific food items each day to enhance your spiritual health and health.

Chapter 1: What Exactly Is Kaballah

It is believed that the Kabbalah (or Qabbalah) is an ancient Hebrew system of spiritual growth created to help you comprehend the universe. It is built in the concept of the Tree of Life which helps explain the universe and also helps you attain enlightenment.

It is believed that the Kabbalah is based on the idea in The Tree of Life. The Tree of Life is comprised of 10 sefirot (the singular is sefirah , and often spelled sephirah) connections on the Tree of Life. There is an 11th that is a sefirah hidden called Da'ath (Westernized) or Da'at (Hebrew).

The process of learning about the Kabbalah involves going between sefirah to sefirah through the paths. The journey from the beginning in the life tree up to the top is a journey to spiritual enlightenment. The many paths and symbols used along the way symbolize spiritual transformations, but they can also be utilized for Ceremonial or High Magic and Kabbalistic Magic.

The Kabbalah can serve as a model of life and the world around you that can be applied to virtually every aspect you can think of. Through Kabbalah we try to understand the essence that is the world, the human existence, and our reason to be here.

To understand the Kabbalah it is necessary to be aware that it's about letting go to the world, rather than being a "me" self-centered, ego-based system.

The word Kabbalah in its translation refers to "that that is received" and in order to receive, you first need to be open and create a vessel within yourself that allows you to absorb the knowledge of the Kabbalah and to understand the ideas in the life tree.

The Kabbalah is the most secretive of Jewish Rabbi's for several years and was the subject of a huge fascination for spirituality in Victorian England the Kabbalah soon moved to the west, which was where it is taught as Ceremonial Magic, and gained significance as a method of spiritual awakening.

All in all, Kabbalah is split into three distinct types:

1. Theoretical is focused on the inner dimensions of the world.

2. Spiritual Worlds, including angels, souls, meditation and much more. The purpose of this course is to help students to attain the highest degree of consciousness and even experience prophecy in connection to the Divine.

3. Magical - it's focused on influencing the natural course of events by using seals, amulets, incantations and god names God and other mystical practices.

The magical aspect of Kabbalah is one of the main reasons it is so well-known in the West and has people such as Dion Fortune and Alistair Crowley advocating Kabbalah as a means that can bring enlightenment and magic. It is a method that could take years or even decades to master and is a source of great potential.

One of the greatest masters of the magical Kabbalah included the Rabbi Joseph Della Reina (1418-1472). As per legends, he sought to make use of his spiritual power to bring about the ultimate redemption, but he hurt himself spiritually. The events that took place to him remain the subject of many legends there are those who say that he was insane, some claim he committed suicide and others claiming that the transformation of his body into a spiritual being.

Whatever was the reason, generations following him stopped studying the magical part of Kabbalah and the knowledge disappeared. The knowledge that has been revived from the Victorian spiritualists isn't based entirely on Jewish tradition, with the majority in it being modernized interpretations the ancient wisdom.

The meditative component of Kabbalah is not completely gone off. But, since the advent of Kabbalistic Zen centers of the West (symbolized by the red thread that is worn around the wrist, and embraced by stars like Madonna) the practice is now more well-known because people are seeking the meaning of their lives. Meditation on the Kabbalah could lead to tranquility and awakening and help you achieve the state of being more conscious.

A lot of the works written on the subject of Kabbalah are inspired by the theoretical aspects of it. The most important research on the theory of Kabbalah can be found in the Zohar which is the doctrines of the Talmudic mystic named from Rabbi Shimon Bar Yochai, who was alive at the end of the 2nd century following Christ. His teachings were spread via word of mouth until they were published near the middle of the 13th century . Rabbi Moshe De Leon.

In the past, the study of the study of the theoretical Kabbalah can be divided into three periods:

1. The Publication of The Zohar - the early lessons of the Kabbalah

2. The 16th Century Mystics of the period (many hailing from Safed) performed a great deal of work using the Kabbalah which led to what is now known as the huge Kabbalistic Renaissance.

3. The Chassidic movement, founded by Baal Shem Tov (1698 until 1760)has had a profound influence on mystical movements, and continues to do so indirectly in the present.

If you don't aren't familiar with the Kabbalah thoroughly, it may appear to be an odd and fantastical picture that is unrelated to the actual world. When you begin to dig into the Kabbalah but you'll gradually begin to understand that this is a complex subject that you might not be able to master even after all of your life.

It is believed that the Kabbalah is a largely poorly understood system One of the most commonly held beliefs being that it will provide psychic abilities. The reason you should study Kabbalah Kabbalah is to enhance your abilities and to improve your understanding of the universe. For those who want to be a part of the wisdom of it, studying Kabbalah can lead to spiritual awakening and connection with God.

For many studying Kabbalah is an effort of an entire lifetime. It can be an obsession once you understand how deep and important it truly is. With many thousands of years of history, study and traditions, there are vast amounts of information regarding the Kabbalah and how to make use of it to change yourself or your lifestyle.

The study of the Kabbalah isn't just about studying the book. It's about practicing it out according to the Kabbalistic principles and implementing your life according to the Kabbalah along with its teachings on a daily basis. Doing otherwise would be the same as trying to feel love through studying a book about it. You could become an expert in the field of literature, but you'll not truly understand what it is like until you experience it.

The inability to live the Kabbalah in your studies can be like trying to comprehend a city simply by looking at an outline of the city. If you don't go to the city, discover it to feel the "pulse," you will never fully grasp the meaning behind it. Kabbalah is similar in this as it is a matter of having to be a part of it in order for yourself to be able to sense its pulse, and to comprehend it.

The majority of literature on the Kabbalah is not focused on changing the Self The majority of it is focused on the concept as well as the understanding Kabbalistic The Tree of Life. The majority of Chassidic writings take this idea and incorporates it into your daily life by gaining a better comprehension of the higher paths and the spheres.

Contrary to many self-improvement methods that are based on self-improvement, the Kabbalah does not sweep negativity or negative characteristics under the rug. It scolds them and acknowledges the existence of them, but doesn't give into these. Instead, the way of thinking is completely different, and you are not able to how to fight negativity or overpower it with positive energy.

When you study the path of Kabbalah it is possible to awaken into The Ein Sof, which is the eternal The Divine or God or whatever you'd prefer to label it. When you discover the mysteries of Kabbalah and begin to understand that the sense of separation from the spiritual source is just a figment of our imagination as you're part of that divine total. When you understand this concept whether you are conscious or unconscious it will help you overcome your negative characteristics and emotional reactions.

Three negative characteristics in Kabbalah three negative traits: anger, stubbornness and haughtiness All of them have their roots in the self-image. For an Kabbalist the ego is the root of everything negative. The false notion of self or ego is the basis of all corruption. You are left in a condition created to support it in its survival.

The ego is the source of negative emotions. So when you are angry, it's the self-consciousness of the ego expressing that it's not happy. Fear of destruction fuels the ego, while anger along with other negative feelings are manifestations of your concern with these false assumptions regarding survival. The source of all your negative emotions is your totality of your involvement in this fantasy.

In getting rid of the false perception of self and ego you will be able to conquer your negative feelings. Learning about Kabbalah can help you realize that this false ego that is a façade to hide your eternal soul. When you study the Kabbalah and realize the fact that Ein Sof is all that exists. You experience it not only at a global level, as well as on a personal individual level. Your illusion of being separate disappears as do the negative feelings which are caused through the expression of your self-image.

However, this doesn't mean that you must view your ego as a threat to conquer and conquer. It will be clear to you in your studies that only light Light is real, while that everything else is a way to conceal your truth. This information will help you overcome the negative and grasp the meaning of Kabbalah.

It is believed that the Kabbalah is a deeply important subject, and the issue "What does it mean to be a Kabbalah" is a question which mystics as well as Rabbis have been searching for answers for millennia. When you read this book, you'll gain a deeper understanding of this mysterious method of self-knowing and begin learning ways to incorporate it into your own life.

Aspects of Kabbalah

In terms of the doctrines of Kabbalah are relevant, there are fundamental theological differences in Judaism as well as Kabbalah. Keep in mind that there are distinct similarities connect them and if something seems like they do to you there's an obvious reason why. But it's crucial to emphasize that there was a distinct divergence between the two beliefs and you'll certainly be amazed at the things that make Kabbalah distinctive. Without more delay, let's look at what is what makes Kabbalah so fascinating complicated, complex and controversial religion in all over the world.

God Heard and Hidden:

Kabbalah affirms that two aspects of God must be reconciled to us , and we must be able to comprehend. Ein Sof is what they refer to God is a divine essential essence that is absolute in its transcendence, and is unlimited as well as not able to be understood. In the end, the divine is beyond our comprehension and the divine being is also inaccessible when we try to comprehend the motives and realities that God has for us. This is referred to as the hidden God that places us at a significant disadvantage as humans who are in God's service. God. We are unable to be aware of, or predict the things God will do, or why God does what he does or how we contribute to God's plan of action.

But, there's another option alternative, a different side of the coin, which you may find useful in understanding. There is an expression of God that is made visible to us all through the persona we think of as God. To be able to comprehend and see what God desires through the world which is all around us. The way God interacts with us is another way that to understand and perceive the Revealed God however, by these acts let us know what God the Revealed God is seeking to accomplish. But, we should also be aware to remember that the Revealed God represents the vision which he would like us to be able to see, and it is important to recognize that this aspect of God is a clear indication of his motives and intentions in addition.

It is in this hidden God that a large portion of Kabbalah discovers its fascination and fascination, even as most of Judaism is devoted to researching the revealed God that they acknowledge. The authenticity of this concealed God and the purpose they seek to find out and comprehend is never in doubt this is what makes Kabbalists always question, research and search for more information.

At the heart of every religion is the understanding and interpretation of the absolute authority of the universe. According to Kabbalah it is the only God who hides as well as displays the face of his children and it is the way the God reveals his face is what makes us most curious about his character. The concept of a dualistic God with an established plan of how God interacts with his creation is what makes this God appear to be a bit intimidating initially, and difficult to fully comprehend. We are in a disadvantage, but Kabbalah is awed by this character of God and elaborates on it.

Ten Sefirot: The Ten Sefirot:

When it comes to understanding both the concealed God and the revealed God both are revealed through ten attributes known as the Sefirot. Each of these ten characteristics are used to explain the things God would like to see from his people, and what God is able to reveal God through creation as well as his actions and through the way he speaks to us through prophetic instruction. Each of these attributes are essential to comprehension and ability to grasp God and the hidden secrets and mystical power God has for all of us.

The Sefirot are the most easily comprehended to be explained by Kabbalah through drawing an analogy with and the Tree of Life and several other mysterious analogies that Kabbalah contains. If you search for Kabbalah it is likely to discover a picture of ten circles that appear like a tree. This is the explanation for the Sefirot and also a tool to explain it to them.

I'm going to devote an hour or so in each of these ten characteristics because they are essential to understand God and the way Kabbalists deal with spiritual issues.

Let's take a look to understand the concept more clearly.

Keter:

Keter is sometimes referred to as the crown The reason for this is due to the obvious fact that it can be worn over the head. Therefore, in sense, Keter is an explanation of all things that are above the mind and cannot be understood. This is all that is above our comprehension. This is the nature of the hidden God and the truth that there is a lot something else that we'll never know the solution to. It is the abstract type of concepts that we're not in a position to grasp, touch or express with assistance. It is the basic rumblings that we encounter which we gnash at without understanding them. Because Ketere is the very first on the list, it's also the most sacred and most awe-inspiring of them.

Chokhmah:

Chokhmah is also known as wisdom and is the very first ability of conscious intelligence in Creation in all its forms and is the beginning of existence. It is typically connected to the right eye or right hemisphere of the brain. If you can enhance the ability to do this and increase its effectiveness, then Chokham has two faces. The one is Abba Ila'ah, also known as The Higher Father and the other one is Yisrael Saba, also known by the name of Elder. The end result is that it is pushing you to develop the ability to take a closer look at the reality of things and abstractions until you are able to be able to determine the truth of the matter. This is the fundamental power behind the creative process since you require wisdom and a clear understanding of something before you're able to unleash it fully.

Binah:

An alternative for Chokhmah is Binah that is linked in the eyes of left as well as the left brain. Binah is referred to as something more intricate, for instance, being able to see the potential of the things you see. It is that feeling that you feel and your capacity to consider things. It's the capacity to examine truth after it is discovered , and then take apart Creation to determine what it really means. From Chokhmah Binah increases and analyzes the wisdom that is learned and what truths are discovered all over the world. It is possible to process and transform the wisdom has been revealed to us to be more powerful and substantial than we initially thought. Binah is also connected to women in the universe, and that includes women. If one is fully developed Binah the Binah is also a dual aspect of its existence.

Imma Ila'ah, also called the Mother of God Then the lower one, known as tevunah. It is also known as understanding. Both are part of the Imma that is referred to as the mother.

Da'at:

Under and between Chokhmah Between Chokhmah Binah is Da'at. It is sometimes described as an empty slot , or it is referred to as an extension and reflection of the knowledge and wisdom that came from the previous two. This is something you'll really need to learn about as a way of an amplification in the process of learning. Da'at isn't just sefirah, but rather it's a fusion of all sefirahs. It is all firing at the full force, and each cylinder is running at full power. This is the ability to control everything, creating this higher power into something that is an intelligent weapon. All of it works in unison and harmony. Without Da'at, everything is falling out of balance, and everything gets off balance. People are very keen to have Da'at in their lives to ensure that everything is together.

Chesed:

Chesed is often described as something that is similar to kindness, love, or love in relation to Chesed. Instead of coming up with an intellectual meaning Chesed is more an ethics and theological concept that is used to represent the compassionate aspect of the world. Chesed is a cherished part of every Jewish religion, not only Kabbalah as it is a characteristic required by every denomination to restore the world that surrounds us. Through Chesed the whole aspects of Creation can be healed repaired and restored. This is the very first emotional feature of the sefirot in relation to Kabbalah. They want you to are devoted to God with such a degree that you not turn away from Him. They request that you give your children everything they might ever require and do so with affection. It also emphasizes the care and treatment of those who are sick, attending to the needy and offering hospitality to strangers from the world. It also includes a strong call to you to attend to the deceased as well as the need to ensure peace between all the people in the world. That is the belief of God in actions.

Gevurah:

It is the second emotional characteristic of the sefirot as well. Gevurah could be considered to also represent the source of judgment and limit. Gevurah is the ability to be awe-inspiring and an element that is fire. It is the righteous characteristic that requires an improvement in the world in order to correct the injustices which have been imposed on the world. This is God's way of punishing wrongdoers and the wicked people of the world. This is God's wrath , and divine intervention through his punishing. This is the stifling adherence of the laws and the total issue of justice. This is the opposite of Chesed This is the act which is required and commanded by the divine law. It is believed that Gevurah is your capacity to repress your instinctual desire to help someone else when they are not worthy of it and deserve punishment. This is the ability you have to make the world conform to the model by God and to undo the injustices that affect it.

Tiferet:

Tiferet is the ability to bring be able to bring the mercy to the compassion of Chesed and the power of Gevurah together and reconcile the two forces. In this moment, these two forces are both giving and receiving. At the end of the day, this can be described as the mercy of God. This is how compassionate compassion stifles the need of justice as well as punishment. This is how we can cooperate with both. It's an element of the central pillar in the Tree of Life, which signifies that it has the capacity to connect two aspects and disperse them among other traits. It is a reminder the notion that punishment and justice have to be balanced with compassion and love. The two cannot be in conflict and we need to cooperate with them instead of being domineering over the other. Without Tiferet your capacity to keep your emotions in check will be difficult to keep. Being able to do this is essential to comprehend the hidden and the Revealed God.

Netzach:

Netzach is transmuted into eternity, and represents God's perpetuality, victory and perseverance that the Kabbalah calls for to be acknowledged. This is the very first thing we'll discuss called the sefirot tactical. When we talk about the term "tactical sefirot, it refers to its acquisition of another thing. It is a way to understand what's happening around you. You do not look at things the eyes of a person, but rather see them as the way to an final goal they bring. Sefirot is the term used to describe a process which is specifically geared towards man and what is the most effective method for man to gain the wisdom of God. It is about the perseverance and determination to persevere with passion until the goals you set. This is leadership and the ability to gather those who will help you to achieve your goals and inspire them to act in the best interests in God's scheme.

Hod:

Hod means glory, magnificence and glory. It's the method that allows you to be active and reach your objectives. Hod is often compared with your feet, and hands are used to accomplish tasks, Hod helps you accomplish those tasks. Hod is your capacity to manage your issues and conquer them. It's where the structure is given to the words and can be the best way to unravel understanding the puzzle of the form. It's the only way to meet your goals and accomplish your objectives.

Yesod:

Yesod is also known as the foundation. it's the ability you have to comprehend the things you're doing. In the case of Yesod it's about your foundation as well as your understanding and your expertise. It's not only your spirituality, but also the community that you are part of. When you consider the foundations of the world that you live in, it will empower you to make a difference in the world. Consider the it as the foundation of the world around you, and the real existence of Creation within your own life. That's what's likely to change around you. You're working to bring about change surrounding you, in order to restore and save.

Malkuth:

It is the base part of the Tree of Life, and it's the final of the Sefirot meaning that it's the final section we'll be talking about. Malkuth is referred to as the spiritual realm of God which is the ultimate triumph that all of the work is geared towards. It is the wedding ring of God and is the goal of everyone to bring the kingdom of God to the top of the list throughout the world. It will change all things in the world, and will be the power that will change everything. At the very end of it all, it is the foundation of everything else that will develop out of this movement.

Evil and Man's Role Man:

Evil is considered to be an essential aspect of life. It's the thing that will cause conflict with everything you're trying your best to do while involved in the Kabbalah. Evil is not viewed as a threatening force, but as something essential to allow God in order to be able. If it weren't to cause conflict and evil throughout the world, God could not be compared with any other thing. If it weren't for the evils of this world, we wouldn't be able to appreciate God's goodness. God and our desire is to live with him and be in the communion of God. Therefore, if there is an element of evil required, then it's our duty to ensure that we do all that we can to make sure that we are aware that evil will never cease to exist and there will always be evils that are perceived.

The only thing that isn't accepted to be sanctioned by God is the deeds created by humans. As a part of Creation It is our responsibility to become reconciled with God and to learn all possible about God and work hard in order to grow closer to God. Because this isn't in every person's toolkit, we're responsible for righting the wrongs that man commits to the other human beings. According to Kabbalah, it's our duty to ensure that we're in harmony with God and that we're constantly seeking out what we could possibly learn about God.

Reincarnation:

The soul's transmigration is a subject that is common within the Kabbalah circle around the globe. It's known as Gilgul neshamot, or the Cycles of Soul. This is a notion which isn't a lot of a focus in Judaism in the present However, it's an idea that Kabbalists have been embracing for a long time. It's a literary theme and something that many people who study Kabbalah are enthralled by.

There are a myriad of aspects of Kabbalah that you'll find fascinating and fascinating and these are only the beginning. There's a lot of mysticism within Kabbalah that is reflected in the Zohar and other texts people are enthralled by. The more you study Kabbalah and its meaning, the more you'll discover that it's a subject that is extremely complex and deeply. If this has interested you, then I would hope that you'll continue to dig more and more deeply into the subject matter

Chapter 2: Core Kabbalah Concepts

Kabbalists have made it a purpose of demonstrating the difference between hidden and revealed God. Ein Sof, which means "without end" is a reference to the infinite aspects in God that is concealed. This is God The Unknown The Infinite. This means that God is definitely real, but no conclusions regarding God's character are drawn in this passage.

According to Kabbalists they prefer to use the term God as It instead of He. First of all it is because the Hebrew language is devoid of the neuter gender. It is impossible for any word to fully convey or represent "The Infinite" due to God's lofty and majestic nature.

Ein Sof's sole meaning Ein Sof is that God isn't compared with any thing that is known to mankind. In the words of Kabbalists, Ein Sof should never be the reason for your prayers because there is no relationship between the creation with God and Ein Sof.

To become one to the ten components that comprise God's Infinite, Hidden God's being that is known one must have a connection to the ten elements of its nature that are observable. These ten traits are known as the Ten Sephirot that we've previously discussed. Think about it this way: God has two personalities or characteristics. God's infinite Infinite Essence is the most elusive as well as God's ten known attributes.

Sephirot (or sefirot) originally signified "numerals." The word originates from Sefer Yetzirah, or "Book of Formation" among the first Hebrew writings on the significance and character of numbers and letters. The instruments by which God is able to act, or the aspects of God's nature which can be measured, are known as sephirot. Each of the 10 Sephirot is a reference to one of cardinal numbers.

According to some Kabbalists that the word Sephirot originates of the Hebrew root sapper, which translates to "to communicate." In the opinion of Kabbalists who agree with this view that all the aspects or Sephirot show God's character. There has been speculation that

Sephirot originates by Sephirot, which is the Hebrew word sapphire. This is logical since Sephirot could be like precious gems with a radiant glow can illuminate the path of the Kabbalist towards comprehending God.

A lot of people have tried to translate Sephirot into English by referring the Sephirot as "radiances," "spheres," or some other occult term. The Sephirot are often seen as symbolisms for certain aspects of God in the world or God simply being, and all of these are recognizable numerically. The most effective English version of this known God is calculi, which better illustrates the usage of symbols and helps make a decision, however, it is recommended to stick the proper Hebrew phrase, since the Sephirot aren't English concepts.

* The Sephirot This is the One That connects

The Sephirot connects us with the eternal. It serves as a bridge that allows God's unification to remain unquestioned and absolute, while also fostering the connection between the creation and the creator. Therefore, the Sephirot should be the focus to your prayer as an Kabbalist rather than Ein Sof. This distinction is crucial to show that even though you may be in a relationship with God like it is to the conventional notion about God, God remains immaterial eternal, inexplicably, and forever.

If you consider God as a God who tries to make comparisons with physical or emotional attributes of humans the thing you're referring to isn't Ein Sof, but the Sephirot. The description you use of God that suggests an actual body or being able to change or comprise multiple components, is about God as the Sephirot rather than Ein Sof. If you're wondering whether or not Ein Sof is not the God mentioned in the Bible isn't Ein Sof, but the Sephirot. This is why Kabbalists will inform you that there is no reference to Ein Sof within the Bible. The Bible is about the individual, recognizable God but not the infinite, hidden God.

The entire purpose behind Sephirot's concept of Sephirot is to demonstrate the way that both the Infinite as well as the limited be connected. It demonstrates how something that is unknown to all of us is able to be recognized. This Sephirot as well as the Ein Sof link is much as the connection between the soul and the body. Your soul is not visible to you and you don't get to be aware of it in all its aspects although it is the sole possession of your body. You have only 1 soul can see its manifestation through being and actions by how your body moves, breathes and is alive.

The body is the vehicle that your soul uses to live, performs, and manifests itself. It is able to communicate through the channels provided by the body's parts and also through Sephirot. It's not clear how the soul and the body are linked but we do know that there is a soul and it can't be understood fully since it is a part of the body. The same way, Ein Sof is able to move and act through the Sephirot which allows Ein Sof to connect to all of us.

A Mysterious Story

Kabbalah has a long and rich history that has evolved over many stages, and influenced by many beautiful traditions, and inundated with the most amazing stories and secrets that have been passed down from time.

Kabbalah contains a variety of mysteries which have their roots in the many ancient kabbalistic writings written in symbolic form, rituals as well as sacred talismans. These mysteries and secrets should not hinder the aspiring Kabbalist from learning and comprehending the truth of God which is available to you in Kabbalah.

One of the most intriguing aspects of Kabbalah is that, in comparison to any other faith or religion that exists it is the one with a larger, greater knowledge base regarding all things related to the universe and life. Take a look at, if you like the ancient sacred texts that provide specific, detailed information about the structure of an atom, it's shape, the Earth as well as its circular form or the spectrum of the universe of light, parallel universes and many other things. In those ancient manuscripts, which were written long before science was able to prove them and substantiated them, you'll find many truths. Scientists often use the kabbalistic language and terms in conducting their studies. The broad scope of Kabbalah is one of the most intriguing mystery.

For centuries, the quest for the ultimate truth has kept mankind enthralled. We've been through all kinds of mysterious rituals and experienced a variety of personal experiences, yet we keep searching, looking to solve the universe's deepest, darkest and most astonishing mysteries. Many have joined elite groups, intrigued by the idea of finally figuring out the meaning of life that is elusive in the hope of a greater connection to the Divine.

The heart of Kabbalah contains the mystery of understanding the Godhead or the secret of belief, referred to as the raza dimehemanuta. In this mystery, the many other mysteries that must be discovered pour out.

*The Four Worlds of Kabbalah

The Four Worlds, known as Olamos or Olamot (singular form, Olam), is the most fundamental in the realm of spirituality according to Kabbalah in the Existence's ascending chain. According to Kabbalah the downward chain, also known as the hishtalshelut , or seder hishtalshelut is a descent of all spiritual realms and is a form of an encircling chain that originates that descends from Creation as well as God. Every world is its own reality, and was created because of its proximity or distance to divine revelation.

It is possible to think of each dimension as consciousness in its own unique form, which is reflected in the world via the eyes of the soul's psychological process. In some cases, the Four Worlds is considered the Five Worlds, with a world that is prior to the one before it. In essence, The Four Worlds is the Tree of Life divided in four different levels each of which corresponds to sight, speech as well as smell and hearing.

* Atziluth -- The archetypal World

* Beri'ah -* Beri'ah - The Creative World

* Yetzirah - The Formative World

* Asiyah -* Asiyah - The Material World

All of them originate from Ein Sof's creative force that is the Divine Infinite. It is created through the multi-leveled tzimtzum that are way too numerous to mention. Tzimtzum is a word which means "condensation" also known as "contraction" which is also known as "constriction" and is frequently employed within the Lurianic Kabbalah to expand upon the theory that was formulated by Isaac Luria that says the method by which God started his act of creation was by contracting his infinite light, also known as Ohr Ein Sof to create may be a conceptual space that could be a place where universes that are independent and finite could exist. The primary contraction which creates an halal happanuy, or an empty space in which the light of God is able to be seen, is symbolized by the tzimtzum symbol.

The tzimtzum reveals the realm where both physical and spiritual realms can exist, as well as the ability to freely choose. Therefore, in Kabbalah, God is called Ha-Makom. This refers to The Omnipresent or the place. In the

Rabbinic texts, "He is the Place of the World However, it is not His Place. World does not belong to His home." This is an example of a Divine paradox, in which the Divine is at the same time present and absent, not only in the absence of any vacuum but also in the process of Creation.

God is often referred to as the "Most Secret Of All Hidden" in the Zohar. Etymologically speaking, Olam is related to Ha'elem, the term used in the Bible meaning "concealment." Each dimming that creates the various levels of the spiritual realm or world through Sephirot's mediation. This is the way in which all Five Comprehensive Worlds come to be. The higher realms are the manifestations of the greater realization of the Ohr the Divine Light, as they are close to their source existence. Lower realms can also be influenced by the creative flow of The Source but up to an extent. Consider all the realms of the universe as clothes which Ein Sof adorned with. The Hasidism teaches us to consider their existence as a reflection of Creation as the Infinite is all-encompassing from above.

There are Sephirots responsible for every dimension, the fourth which is the original Adam Kadmon is distinguished due to its transcendental nature. It is possible to find the names of the four other realms in the Bible in the chapter of Isaiah chapter 43, verse 7: "Everyone that is called by My name and in My honor (being the Atziluth that is the Emanation or the Close) I have created (Beriah meaning the idea of creation) I have made (Yetzirah which means the process of creation) Even I have created (Asiyah which means the act) following Asiya is the lowest of the spiritual realms The Asiyah-Gashmi or the Physical Asiyah which is our physical World". This is the world that encompasses the last part of the Sephirot emanations and that is, the Yesod as well as the Malchut. In total, based upon their initial letters The Four Worlds are known as ABiYA. Each of the four worlds has a role to contribute to the process of creation and acts as the embodiment of various aspects of consciousness or awareness within the world of life.

* About Enumeration

Ohr Mimalei Kol Olmin is the Divine and creative light that is responsible for the creation of all worlds. It fills every World with the most light it is able to allow. The 10 Sephirot as well as their 12 partzufim , or personae (faces or configurations, or forms, if you like) they make their light appear in every universe, except for Adam Kadmon, for now. They are also more visible in manifesting the Divine.

The partzufim connect all the way as per the Lurianic Kabbalah. The sublime is shrouded within the lower levels hidden as the soul. But, every world is controlled by certain partzufim along with Sephirot.

* Adam Kadmon, which means the Primordial Man. The Yosher Sephirot's upright appearance is represented by Adam the anthropomorphic symbol. The Sephirot assumes Man's unrecognisable shape. Kadmon is a reference to Kadmon, which is the "primary among all

primordialities" as it is the first and purest of the emanations. It's linked to Ein Sof. Adam Kadmon is of the Keter Elyon realm, also known as The Supernal Crown of Will, with the bright and lucid light known as Tzachtzachot. The Sephirot is pure, lucid and veiled with regard to its possibilities. It is part of Creation's future, the emergence of. It is Divine Light which does not have vessels, and is the expression of God's Divine Plan, in the setting of Creation that is extremely specific. The same way, the Keter is regarded as the ultimate Sephirot, Adam Kadmon is thought to be the highest of all other realms and the only reference to Adam Kadmon is made to The Four Worlds, and not Adam Kadmon itself.

* Atziluth is the word used to describe the World of Emanation. It also signifies "close." The meaning of "close" is that Ohr Ein Sof is still shining and remains in close contact to its origin in the world. This is the most amazing revelation, divine emanations and souls are not able to see their own existence within Atziluth. In this case, it's an enlightenment that 10

Sephirot appear. Chochma (wisdom) prevails, and all things are able to negate the essence of Bitul HaEtzem as it relates to Divinity , and is not considered as separate or created. Malchut, which is the last of the sephirah is the symbol of the Divine speech of Genesis Chapter 1 in the Holy Bible, which is the food source for the lower realms.

* Beri'ah is the world of Creation. This is the concept of creation from nothing or creating ex in nihilo. Creation is here without any form or structure. The creatures are aware that they exist however, they do not know of being or existence. Divinity and Bitul HaMetzius. This is the world of the Divine Throne and it shows that the Sephirot shape of Atziluth descending down to Beri'ah as a King on the Throne. Understanding, also known as the sephirah Binah, is the dominant aspect in this. This is often referred to as divine intelligence or the higher Garden of Eden.

* Yetzirah is called the realm of creation. It is at this level that what is created takes shape and form. Yesod and Chesed Both emotional

Sephirot dominate the world today. The angels of the Yetzirah's souls participate in worship through pushing and divine emotion. They are aware of how far they've travelled between themselves as well as the full understanding of Beriah. The Divine energy is channeled through the ascent and descent through the realms. This fulfills the Divine intent.

* Asiyah is the realm of action. It is the culmination of creation thanks to the nature of the Divine vitality. It's still regarded as spiritual. The angels in this area are active Malchut is the king of sephira. Under, Asiyah is the physical Asiyah also known as Asiyah Gashmi The most solitary of worlds that is the physical universe that we inhabit.

The Four Worlds are of the spirit and comprise a long chain which descends. Kabbalah is an examination of the metaphysical. The Ohr is merely an illustration of the Divine Emanation, and the terms "lower" as well as "higher" describe the separation of every world in relation to revelation as well as Divine consciousness.

Ein Sof and the Sefirot

What separates Kabbalah from other types that comprise Jewish mysticism is its doctrine that is based on Ein Sof (the Infinite, inaccessible divine nature) as well as the Sefirot (the divine emanations). Although Kabbalah is fostered by the earlier types of Jewish mysticism and spirituality, the profound consciousness that is the hallmark of Kabbalah can be expressed, and recorded through the unique notions that are the basis of Ein Sof and the Sefirot.

The Infinite One

Kabbalah offers two primary spiritual experiences. One is the belief that God is eternal, transcendent and indestructible. Another one is God is also intimately personal. This means that the exact the same Transcendent one is active and is present throughout Creation. Kabbalah shows these two perspectives by using the words Ein Sof and the Sefirot.

Rabbi Meir Ibn Gabriel explains that we can't comprehend Ein Sof, a term coined in the time of Isaac the Blind meaning literally "without ending," or "infinite"--through reflection or logic. The essence of God is not within our grasp even though we can get an inkling of the real-world reality and appreciate the existence of that which is vastly beyond our comprehension. Ein Sof itself is a negative formula, which means that there isn't a limit. This is like Maimonides explaining that we are able to only define that God is , but not what God is because God is beyond our ability to define. Definitions are a way to restrict the scope of what is possible, while God is infinite. The Kabbalists were aware Ein Sof was beyond words and thought. Ein Sof is beyond language and thought, and therefore it is impossible to speak about it.

Before the Start

Ein Sof is the source of any emanation or Creation. Emanation originates from Ein Sof and brings forth the realm of the Sefirot (Olam HaSefirot). The most well-known poem and prayer dating back to the 11th century "Adon Olam" (meaning the words "Eternal Lord" and "Lord of the Universe" simultaneously] which is attributed to Solomon Ibn Gabirol, contains several phrases that convey the meaning from Ein Sof: "Adon Olam who was the ruler before everything was created , and when the end of all creation [Adon Olamalone] will reign supremely ... with no ever having a beginning or an ending."

Ein Sof is understood as the state of pure divinity that emanates from the source of all creation. It is not a dualistic state in Ein Sof. There is kein "personality" inside Ein Sof. Ein Sof is a total being. Because there isn't any duality and there is no distinction there are no adjectives that can apply to Ein Sof. In the end, everything is part of Ein Sof in some sense.

Divine Will, Creation, and Ein Sof

Many Kabbalists take on the Sefirot the map of their reality, from a philosophical perspective. Many questions were raised for them with regard to Ein Sof, emanation, and the universe of Sefirot. What was the reason Ein Sof created the universe? If emanation was the reason for Creation Did this lessen the quality that is Ein Sof?

There is no clear answer to the question of what brought Ein Sof to the universe. Certain Kabbalists believed in Creation as arising from God's will, and often identified the will of God with Keter which is generally regarded as to be the first Sefira. Will was not believed to be the work of Ein Sof because there are no traits that can be attributed to It. There were many perspectives regarding the question about "will" and the question of which Sefira was the source.

It is essential to understand the fact that Kabbalah has a long history as does Judaism itself. Different Kabbalists are different in their viewpoints, philosophical views and spiritual experiences. Certain Kabbalists tend to be the more "orthodox" than other people, which means that they are less hesitant to adopt a new viewpoint or one that appears to contradict the traditional Jewish beliefs and rituals.

There's Only Ein Sof

Ein Sof is not at any point diminished by the emanation process. A way to describe how the relation with Ein Sof and the emanation can be compared to the two to a flame that lights candles. While the candles draw their light from a larger spark, they're still lit by a fire that does not diminut that initial fire. In the same way, Ein Sof is not diminished in any way by the emanation of Sefirot.

Moshe Cordovero (1522-1570) explained that even though the image of light was utilized in relation to Ein Sof however, it is crucial to keep in mind that Ein Sof isn't "light," however sublime the light might be since light can be a physical object in its own right, and Ein Sof isn't.

in his work Elimah Rabbati, Cordovero gives an excellent argument for Ein Sof in the following section: "Before all emanation, there was only Ein Sof which is all real. Although Ein Sof emanated all that exists, there's the only Ein Sof and nothing outside it. There is no entity that does not have God's power. God in it. If that weren't the case, then you could be limiting God and apologizing for duality. God should not be a part of it. God is all there is However, not all things are God."

The mystical feeling of the unity of God and all that is cannot be expressed in the language of the human mind to communicate. The more philosophical Kabbalists tried to articulate their views of God and the universe using a system of symbolism that was coherent that is known as the Sefirot.

Sefirot's World World of the Sefirot

The development from the Sefirot universe provided a framework to explain the way God can be transcendent and immanent throughout Creation simultaneously. The Kabbalist's vision of the universe as divinely brimming was explained by Emanation. The prophet Isaiah describes this view in the Bible in the passage "The entire universe is filled by God's glory" (Isaiah 6:3). The word "glory" (Kavod) was believed by Kabbalists as an alternative term to the 10th Sefira which is that is, the Divine Presence (Shekhinah).

The Sefirot describe the process of creation that leads from Absolute infinite Divinity (Ein Sof) that exists beyond the boundaries of time to being the creator and the existence of our physical universe that we inhabit. The Sefirot are the manifestations of the Divine which originate from Ein Sof which is the unifying divinity. Their creation is the beginning of a sequence of events which culminates in being the creator of our physical world.

The Term Sefirot: Decoding the Meaning Sefirot

Kabbalists attempted to understand the essence of the term Sefira and, in turn, describe its meaning. Sefer HaBahir, the earliest Kabbalistic text that explains the word using a passage of Psalms: "The Heavens declare M'saprim the glory to God" (19:2). The word M'saprim is derived from similar roots to Sefira. Also, the Sefirot are the method that the hidden essence of God that is hidden inside Ein

Sof, is manifested. The Sefirot in this way proclaim the "glory" to God.

Another word with the same root Sefira, sappir, is also used to describe the meaning of Sefirot. Sappir is an example of a sapphire. The explanation offered is that just like the sappir's light shines through many different angles, even though it is only one stone, the Sefirot sparkle by divine "light" with a myriad of facets is too. They are one. The sappir was one the twelve stones found in the breastplate of the high priest.

Are Sefira an Hebrew word or is it a Greek word?

The word Sefira is not derived from a similar Greek phrase, sphaira, that means "sphere." Its meaning is one that is a Hebrew one. However, the word gematria is a reference to the numeral value of letters is a word borrowed from Greek.

Beginning with Ein Sof to the Physical Universe

There are a variety of distinct patterns and distinctions which are crucial in the realm of Sefirot. Each Sefira has less divine power in the sense that the Sefira "descends" out of Ein Sof. The infinite heavenly "light," known as Or Ein Sof, is decreasing. In another way the upper Sefira is comprised of all the lower ones, while each following Sefira is made up of all the above, but in reduced form.

The symbols of Sefirot

The Kabbalists who specialized in the realm of Sefirot came up with an extensive and intricate symbol system. The Sefirot system is prevalent throughout Theosophical Kabbalah with some variation but mostly with a great degree of coherence. The way things were conducted changed significantly with the advent of Isaac's Kabbalistic system, prior to that the method by the manner in which Sefirot could be discussed had been identical for many centuries.

The Ten Sefirot in descending order in their expression of Ein Sof are as follows:

* Keter (crown)

* Chokhmah (wisdom)

* Binah (understanding)

*Hesed (loving-kindness) (also known as Gedulah (greatness)

* Gevurah (power) or Din (judgment)

* Tiferet (beauty) or Rakhamim (compassion/mercy)

* Netzach (eternity or victory)

* Hod (splendor)

* Yesod (foundation)

* Malkhut (Kingdom) or Shekhinah (Divine Presence)

Divergent configurations of the Sefirot

The dynamics of Sefirot are categorized and explained in a variety of ways. One approach is to divide these into three column: left, right and middle. The right is an essence that is Hesed and is believed to be filled with love. The left is the embodiment of strength (Gevurah) and judgement (Din). Both of these parts depend on one another. With no boundaries, the love of God is overwhelming and has no boundaries. However it is impossible to resist the power of pure judgement. The existence of things requires both two forces, with one tempered by the other. Middle column represents the combination of the two forces. The result of the synthesis between Hesed along with Gevurah is known as Tiferet (beauty) that is often referred to in the form of the word Rakhamim (compassion/mercy). It is said to be a Midrash which states that many universes existed prior to the one that we currently exist. The other universes could not be sustained because the ideal equilibrium among Din and Hesed was not yet attained.

The Ten Sefirot

Another way to divide the Sefirot is to divide it into three sets composed of three triangles. The first set includes Keter, Chokhmah, and Binah which represent the precursors to the emanation. Next include Hesed, Gevurah, and Tiferet. The final three Netzakh, Hod, and Yesod and Yesod, all ending in Shekhinah which is the entrance via which Shefa (divine power) is released into the physical world.

Seven lower Sefirot are usually separated from the three upper ones. These lower Sefirot are frequently called "the Building" (Binyan in Hebrew). They also represent the beginning days of Creation according to Genesis. Each Sefira is a different day in Creation. On the seventh day Shabbat The most sacred day in the entire week coincides with Shekhinah which is the feminine Divine Presence The Sefira closest and the most accessible to the physical universe.

By observing Shabbat and Shabbat, an occasion that is more devoted to "being" instead of "doing," we may get closer to the Divine Presence and the Shekhinah. Shabbat was also referred to as Shabbat HaMalka Shabbat, the Sabbath Queen as well as the "Bride" that were direct reference to its relationship with the Shekhinah.

YHVH along with it's World of the Sefirot

The whole world of Sefirot was believed to be represented by the God's specific name the name YHVH. The smallest letter of the alphabet, yud, is the first letter in the name and is a symbol of Chokhmah (knowledge) which is the moment of clarity. Chokhmah develops in Binah's "womb," which is an expansion of knowledge which is a nurtured moment of clarity. The first hey of YHVH symbolizes Binah the mother of the universe. In Hebrew "hey" is a letter used to end the feminine singular words.. The word vav, which is second in Name is the symbol for the following six Sefirot. Vav is a gematria that's six. In addition, the final hey in YHVH is symbolic of Shekhinah the second Mother/Bride/Queen who gives birth to the universe created by creating Shefa.

Two Biblical verses (Psalm 110:10, and Proverbs 4.7.1) the expression "reshit Chokhmah" can be found. It literally translates to "the the beginning of wisdom" however the Kabbalists believed that it was "reshit is chokhmah. This interpretation is plausible since "is "is" does not exist in Hebrew however it is understood in the context of the phrase. So both interpretations of reshit the word chokhmah could be possible.

As Chokhmah is known as Reshit (beginning) and is the beginning of the world, it's appropriate to note that YHVH starts by introducing the yud which represents Chokhmah But what happened with Keter (crown) within the depiction? The yud usually appears with a tiny point towards the top, which is pointed upwards. The tip is what "crowns" it is a symbol of, or points towards, Keter.

Where do the names of the Sefirot originate?

Some of the names used by the Sefirot originate from a passage in the Bible from Chronicles I: "Yours, YHVH is the greatness Gedulah and Power of Gevurah as well as The Beauty of Tiferet as well as the victory/eternity [Netzakh] as well as the glory [Hod] for all that exists both in Heaven and on earth Yours is the Kingdom" (29:11).

The Cosmic Tree

The entire universe of Sefirot is usually arranged in two ways that is the trees or Adam Kadmon, the primordial human. The tree's symbol that is seen in Sefer HaBahir has been flipped upside down (its roots are above, and its branches are on the bottom). "The "roots" in the trees, naturally are the most heavenly Sefirot that ultimately originate out of Ein Sof.

Pardes along with The Garden of Eden

The symbol of the tree has it a connection to Pardes or the orchard that is a symbol to communicate mystical experiences and wisdom. It also makes a connection with two trees that are mentioned in the Genesis account in the Garden of Eden, the Tree of Life and the Tree of Knowledge of good and evil. It is believed that the Tree of Life itself is linked to The Sefirot and the Sefirot of Tiferet (beauty) also known as Yesod (foundation) The Tree of Knowledge is also associated with the Sefirot of Tiferet (The Tree of Knowledge is connected to Shekhinah (the Divine Presence).

The calendar has four New Year's in the Jewish calendar. The most popular is Rosh Hashanah, which falls in October or September, in celebration of Creation. The 15th day of the Hebrew sh'vat month (called Tu B'Sh'vat) is the New Year for trees, that became a major festival for Kabbalists due to the tree symbolism within the Sefirot.

Kelipot Blocking Divine Energy

The tree's bark acts as "kelipah," which refers to the outer layer that blocks God's "light" from entering. The concept of the kelipot (plural of the word kelipah) hindering the divine flow is essential to the Kabbalistic worldview. There were a variety of opinions about the concept of kelipot. Certain Kabbalists believed in the kelipot as ten and others believed that there were four. They took from the opening chapter in Ezekiel's Vision (1:4). The first three Kelipot are fundamentally evil, while the fourth one has the potential to be good or evil according to our actions. It is similar to the existence both good and bad on the Tree of Knowledge.

Adam Kadmon: The Human Primordial Adam Kadmon

The other major symbol of Sefirot is Adam Kadmon. Sefirot universe is Adam Kadmon, the primordial human that is both male and female in the same being. Each Sefira is a different part of the body on this map of symbolic Sefirot. The head is depicted by the three first Sefirot, Hesed by the right arm and Gevurah through the left arm. The body is Tiferet and the left leg represents Netzakh while the leg on left is Hod. Male sexual organ Yesod, female sexual organ Malkhut.

Genesis (1:27) refers to humans as being made by God. It isn't the nature to the Bible to state a fact that is then followed by a discussion in this way. Because of this absence of explanation, comments regarding the meaning of the phrase are abundant. For Kabbalists it is the Adam Kadmon representation from the realm of Sefirot is the most accurate reason.

Metaphors and Anthropomorphism for God

Although the Bible is filled with human-like representations, such as God's "hand" and "voice" that is God, Judaism generally insists that God is a solely "spiritual" being, and has no physical attributes. This is made clear in Maimonides within the Thirteen Principles of Faith, in which he argues that all these physical descriptions are metaphors. The Talmud states it is because "[t]he Torah spoke in the human language" (Tractate Brakhot 31a) which means in a way that humans could comprehend. A passage taken from Isaiah, "To whom can you be comparing God?" (40:25) is frequently used as evidence of the fact that God is a God of an entirely different kind from any other thing in existence.

The various names for God have been associated with various Sefirot. Names like Ehyeh is linked to Keter and the name Adonai (as it actually pronounced aleph, dalet or nun, the word yud) that literally means "my Lord"" is associated with Shekhinah and Shekhinah; and the name YHVH and all the Sefirot all.

The Kabbalists tend to stress and reiterate that even though they employ a very visual, physical language in order to communicate with God and God's attributes, they're communicating symbolically. God is inexhaustible, which means that God is not a physical entity. However visually-based language allows Kabbalists Kabbalists to express their thoughts in a less abstract manner than it could otherwise be. It is also the case with the Bible. The Bible has a strong emotional impact partly because it imparts its message through stories, and makes use of a language that is very real and can affect the readers in a way which abstract thought isn't capable of.

God's "Image"

The representation of Adam Kadmon makes every human to be a symbol for Divinity. Our actions in a flash are seen as a reflection of God's presence in the world. Every person we see is not just an individual, but also an emblem for the universe of Sefirot and the expression "in my flesh I will behold God" (Job 19:26) is given new meaning.

The concept of kelipot takes on emotional and psychological implications. We can see our own internal struggles as kelipots obstructions to connecting to God and our divine nature. While the Kabbalists are careful to emphasize that God is completely spiritual, the picture of Adam Kadmon gives an entirely new meaning to the notion that human beings are made by God.

Shiur Komah

Shiur Komah, a text which outlines the measurements of God's stature, was among of the first forms of Jewish mysticism. The descriptions regarding God's Divine Body were huge in their scope that they appear to highlight how absurd physical description of God. People who were against mysticism in the Jewish tradition were frequently skeptical of the work. However, Kabbalists considered it one of the greatest mysteries of mysticism and experiences. Although the word Shiur Komah remains used, its meaning changed throughout the centuries. The concept of Adam Kadmon as a symbol of the world of Sefirot corresponds to the more modern significance that is Shiur Komah.

So Above, so Below

Kabbalists study the Torah at a variety of levels. The events mentioned in the literal sense in the Torah text can be seen as being a reference to the events that took place within the divine realms as well as between human beings as well as the Divine. Kabbalists believe that the characters in the biblical narratives as a symbol of different realms of reality. Abraham for instance, is not just the human character depicted in Genesis as well as an incarnation for The Sefira in Hesed. Battles like that with Amalek the tribe which took on Abraham and the Jewish girls and women in the back following the Exodus from Egypt is symbolic of the epic conflict between good and evil.

For an Kabbalist scriptures, the Torah may have multiple interpretations at once. At the "sod" ("Secret," mystical) level of the text, for instance there is no reason to preclude others, even if they seem to be different. The literal interpretation of Scripture is not negated, but it does exist it often takes a back place to the mystical interpretation that is regarded as "the way to truth."

Kabbalists also see Creation as a symbol and see that the 7 days of Creation as the manifestation of the previous seven Sefirot and are known as Binyan (the construction). Shabbat is the seventh day in the weekly calendar, has been which is associated with Shekhinah. Kabbalists believe that Shabbat as the time when the Divine Presence is at its most readily available and when humans are on a spiritual level. Every human action, no matter how simple it appears at first glance, is crucial according to the Kabbalistic worldview as God's energies (Shefa) is influenced by our actions. This has given tremendous energy to the traditional Jewish daily life.

Chapter 3: The Sefer Yetzirah

The Sefer Yetzirah is the Book of Creation or the Book of Formation. It is one of the first writings about Jewish mysticism. Many thought of it as more of a treatise on mathematical and linguistic theories and not Kabbalah.

Yetzirah refers to "formation," while Briah is "creation." The patriarch Abraham is the one who is acknowledged for the book. Some people attribute the book as being the product of Rabbi Akiva . The scholars of our day and age have yet to reach consensus on the source to the Sefer Yetzirah. Rabbi Saadia Gaon claims that the main point that the author of the book wanted to prove was how the world around us was created.

The book starts with a description of how God created everything making use of his 32 "mysterious paths of wisdom." The book says that the various derivatives of the word Sefer made the world:

* Sefer - A Book

* Sefor -* Sefor -

"* Sippur" -- A tale

God also took into account the measurement of space that was empty and a major part of the creation process was the 22 alphabet letters in Hebrew with three primary letters as well as seven consonants or double sounding letters along with twelve normal letters.

* The Origin of the Sefer Yetzirah

There's a tale you will find inside the Babylonian Talmud that talks about how prior to every Shabbat, Rav Hoshaiah, and Rav Hanina would gather together and read in the Sefer Yetzirah while making a delicious calf that they would consume. According to many mystics Abraham of the Bible did exactly the same while preparing the calf for angels that had let him know of Sarah's imminent child, as mentioned it is mentioned in Genesis Chapter 18, verse 7.

The appendix to the Sefer Yetzirah clarifies that Abraham was the one who received the mystic lore through a revelation from the Divine. This is why classic rabbis and philosophers such as Shabbetha Donnolo Saadia Gaon as well as

Judah HaLevi are of the strong belief That the sefer yetzirah's source is the sole responsibility of Abraham. Rabbi Akica has simply altered it to the current form. Jewish Lore says that it was the work of Adam Then it was passed down through Adam to Noah and through Noah to Abraham which is also known as Abraham as the Abraham, who is the friend of God. According to a document stored at the British Museum, the Sefer Yetzirah is also known as the Kilkot Thoughzirah and is accessible only to truly religious people.

* Dates the Sefer Yetzirah

Modern historians don't have a solid idea of the source of the text, and they argue about this issue in a heated debate. Some scholars believe that it was written in the middle ages. Some believe it was prior to that time, as a result of the various traditions that pop in the text. But, many contemporary scholars believe that the text was written in the Talmudic period.

According to the Jewish Encyclopedia says that the Sefer Yetzirah's fundamental elements resonate to the 3rd century or possibly the 4th century, too. It is believed to have been written in the Geonic period and could have been crafted following the pattern of Jewish gnosis, which became inactive at the end of the 4th century as long as it hadn't already become extinct by this point.

Richard August Reitzenstein places the Sefer Yetzirah at the time of two centuries BCE. Christopher P. Benton says that the structure of the Hebrew grammar is more likely to mean that it was composed during the Mishnah time period, around in the 2nd century BCE. It is also important to noting that the division the Hebrew alphabet into three classes is evident within Hellenic texts. The only thing that is certain is that the origin and date of the book cannot be determined but they are not yet.

*The Sefer Yetzirah Manuscripts

* The Full Version

* The Short Version

*The Gra Version

*The Saadia Version

Apart from these four variations, there are other versions available. There are only a few variations between these versions.

The shorter version of the Sefer Yetzirah is only 1300 words, whereas it's Long Version is about two times as long. Abraham Abulafia, in the 13th century, noted that both versions are in existence. At the time of 10th century Saadia Gaon was the author of an account in which he discussed the manuscript which was more organized from The Longer Version. The version we have today is known in the Saadia Version. It was in the sixteenth century that Isaac Luria made a revision of the Short Version to bring it into harmony to the Zohar. The redaction was further modified through Vilna Gaon, also known as the Gra of the 18th century, resulting in what is now called the Gra Version.

*The Sefer Yetzirah's Influences

It is believed that the Sefer Yetzirah is dedicated to any speculation or questions regarding how God created the universe through the Divine.

The fact that it is attributed to patriarchal Abraham is proof that the book is considered to be of the highest respect for a long time. It is possible to say that this book had the biggest impact over Jews more than the other book , aside from the Talmud.

It is said that the Sefer Yetzirah is very difficult to comprehend due to the fact that it is an obscure text written in a sloppy style. Further complicating matters is the fact that it is not a critical edition and the majority of the text has been modified. There are, of course, many opinions regarding the source and age, as well as the value and content that comprise Sefer Yetzirah. Sefer Yetzirah.

In the past, it is said that the Sefer Yetzirah is one of the most intriguing of recorded Jewish literature. Apart from the Bible there is no other book that is as rich in annotations like this one. There's a strong relationship to the Sefer Yetzirah as well as the later mystics. There is a distinct difference among both the Sefer Yetzirah in comparison to the modern Kabbalah in it's the fact that Kabbalistic sephirot does not match the one from Sefer Yetzirah. Sefer Yetzirah. It is believed that the Sefer Yetzirah's concept is among of the earliest and clearest connections that can be seen in Kabbalistic concepts' growth and expansion. Instead of creating ex-nihilo the two works both suggest that the existence of mediums that took place in a sequence that connected the universe with God. They also both view the source of the universe to be God instead of assuming God is the sole and efficacious creator of all things.

There's a book called Sefer Yetzirah that was circulated throughout the Ashkenazi hasidim between the 11th century and the 13th century. It was later one of the primary sources of Practical Kabbalah. The text is an esoteric work that expands on the concept of the seven days of creation and is similar in some ways to Seder Rabbah deBereshit, which is a minor midrash.

The Structure and Teachings of Seer Yetzirah

The Sefer Yetzirah clearly describes the creation of the Universe by one God that is, that is, the

God of Israel with the "32 amazing techniques that are wisdom."

* The Ten Numbers (the Sephirot)

There are 22 letters in the Hebraic alphabet

* The three Mother Letters (Aleph, Mem, and Shin)

*The 7 Doubles (Bet Gimel, Bet, Dalet, Kaph, Pe, Resh, Taw)

*The 12 elements, or basics (He, Waw, Zayin, Heth, Teth, Yodh, Lamedh, Nun, Samekh, Ayin, Tsade, Qoph)

These divisions align well with Jewish ideas such as the 3 letters that compose God's name, Yud, He, and Vav. They also align to the Jewish week the 12 tribes of Israel, as well as the Hebrew calendar's 12 month calendar, and scientific or philosophical concepts such as the 4 elements (Earth water, air and air) and the 10 , directions and the seven planets as well as the 12 zodiac significations as well as the human function and the different parts of the human body.

This book gives a precise explanation of the way God used all the Hebrew alphabets and the sephirot combing them in various ways to create creation. The book also describes the method by which God disclosed this entire secret to Abraham, the patriarch. Abraham through an covenant. It includes two elements:

*The covenant that is circumcision, or the mila (meaning the word) is found between the 10 toes.

*The covenant between the tongue, or lashion (meaning the word "language") is formed between the 10 fingers.

God then links Abraham's tongue with the 22 letters in the Torah This is how the secret is disclosed to Abraham's patriarch.

* Themes from the Sefer Yetzirah

The macrocosm comprises the universe and the microcosm is yours. In of the Sefer Yetzirah system, they are the different combinations of mystical symbols. They are used by Jewish for the purpose of creating their Holy Name to perform magic or perform miracles with Thaumaturgy requires magic papyri that cite an Angelic Book of Moses, filled with references to names found in the Bible.

The linguistic theories are found inside the Sefer Yetzirah play a key aspect of its philosophy along with Gnostic Cosmogony and Astrology. Aleph, Mem, and Shin aren't just the three mothers that birth the letters that remain in the alphabet, they are the three elements that are primordial, and the core of life.

The Sefer Yetzirah explains that the first manifestation of the spirit of the One was the ruach, which means the air or spirit. This is what made water and the beginning of the fire. In the beginning the three essential substances were the only possible in nature. They didn't even be born before Aleph Mem as well as Shin made them real. Because the letters of mother form an essential part of our language, these three elements are the basic elements upon which the universe was constructed.

The universe is composed of three major components: The World and the Time and the human. They are mingled so that they let all three fundamental elements to exist inside each one. The earth was created by water. Heaven was formed out of fire. The ruach made the air between world and earth.

Here are some other connections that make a difference.

* Summer: The human head

* Winter: Ruach, or the torso

"Rain": Rain, or other body parts.

The seven apertures (ears nostrils, mouths and eyes) are in sync with your seven apertures (mouth, ears, nostrils and eyes) as well as 7 planets. These letters' pronunciation aren't easy. They're also not too hard. The same way, the planets are departing from the earth, while drawing closer to it. The weeks of the week are a reflection of the 7 double letters, and they alter based on the location they're in relation to the seven planets. Your eyes, mouth nostrils, noses, and ears connect you to the outside world. The same is true for the seven planets that connect Above as well as Below.

The 12 zodiac signs form an analogy to the simple 12 letters. All of them are linked to the 12 months and the 12 leaders are the intestines, liver, pancreas, stomach, kidneys, galls, and feet. The body is composed of elements that are not linked chemically, but capable of causing the change of one another at an physical scale.

*The Sefer Yetzirah is a reference to Creation

The book talks about the concept of double creation. One creation is true, while the other one is ideal. The Sephirot aren't real, they're ideal. The numbers 2-10 are the manifestations of number 1 and, in the same manner they are Sephirot originate from the One. They are God's will that is in motion. It is air, and then water and finally fire, which isn't far from the sky. There are also 22 letters that we should consider which are the basis of the world and makes the Sephirot real. The Talmud states that the universe was made up of letters.

There are 32 Paths That Ein Sof engraves

"The letters 22 The real

"* The Ten Sephirot The perfect

The letters can not appear on their own, and they're not forms. The bridge that connects nature and form is used to create the world of reality.

Contrasts

The book explores the natural contrast or the syzygies, or pairs in Gnosticism. The world is made up of pairs that are at war, however are brought together with Ein Sof. For example water and fire are brought to harmony by the air. This is in accordance with the three principals:

* Shin that hushes

*Mem which means mute.

The Aleph is a fusion that brings together Shin and Mem

Here are the seven Contrasts Humans have to deal with every day

* Peace in the face of war

* Wealth against poverty

* Wisdom against foolishness

Beauty versus ugly

* Leadership versus servitude

* Infertility and fertility

* Life versus death

Evil and good aren't considered to be real. There is nothing morally good or negative in its own right but it is how an object affects you with contrast lets you make the decision. We are free to make our own choices and are rewarded or punishment depending on the choices we make. Heaven isn't mentioned but pursuing an ethical path will result in things going in our favor. Being a horrible person who is content with being evil only causes life to pour more energies at us.

* The Phonetic System

The letters of 22 are organized by the organs of vocalization which are involved in their pronunciation and the intensity of their pronunciation. The letters in these five groups have a distinct mode of articulate. But they all have a unique sound. Sefer Yetzirah states that sound cannot be produced by the tongue alone and the speech organs serve to aid in assisting. In that mind, let's take a look at the way that letters are formed.

* Use your tongue and your throat, as well as the end of your tongue

* The point of your tongue, and between your lips

In the middle of your tongue

The upper part of your tongue

* Through your tongue stretched flat, and also by your teeth

The letters are also distinct due to the intensity of the sound for their production is. Below are the subdivided alphabets in accordance with this criteria:

* Mutes: They have no sound as does Mem.

* Sibilants: They are called the hissing Shin similar to Shin.

* Aspirates: They are situated between the sibilants and mutes, similar to Aleph that is light as it "holds that balance between the two."

* Gnostic Systems

It is believed that the Sefer Yetziah is very similar to certain elements of Gnosticism. In the Gnostic Marcus splits the Greek alphabet into three classes, similar to the way it is the case that Sefer Yetzirah splits the Hebrew alphabet into three classes. In Gnosticism the three classes represent symbolisms for the power of three comprising all the upper elements.

Both Seefer Yetzirah and Gnosticism put the emphasis on the power inherent in the many combinations and variations of the letters to describe the beginning and development of multiples that originate from to the One source. This Sefer Yetzirah also lines up with the Clementine doctrine that says that God is the source and the ultimate end of everything that exists. The Clementine writings also declare that God's spirit was transformed into pneuma and from there , into water, then the fire and rocks. This is consistent to the Sefer Yetzirah, which says God's spirit, water fire as well as Earth are the four first of the Ten Sephirot.

In contrast, the other six Sephiroth are just a restricted space-bound by three dimensions that are oriented twofold. The same is true of Clementina which states that it is said that the Divine is the limit of the entire universe as well as the source of all six dimensions.

It is believed that the dragon can also refer to"the" or "curled dragon" (coiled similar to serpents) is an important figure in Sefer Yetzirah's astrology interpretation probably because it is an extremely ancient symbol in Semitism. The dragon is regarded being the Draco constellation. It is an analogy to the cosmic axis that is the south and north poles, as the Draco constellation wraps in the North star and it is also the celestial line. Draco is in contact with the most northern portion of the celestial sphere.

Chapter 4: The Zohar

It is the Sefer Ha-Zohar is also known as the Book of Radiance. It is said in the Bible, "Zohar" appears in a vision of the prophet Ezekiel (Ezekiel Chapter 8 Verse 2) The word "Zohar" is often translated to mean "light" as well as "radiance." The word is also used within the Book of Daniel Chapter 12 verse 3 in which it says, "those who are wise will shine as bright as the light of the sky."

Zohar Zohar was written by hand in Aramaic and is an esoteric and mystical commentary on Torah. It is composed of multiple volumes that add up to more than 1,000 pages. The Zohar comprises a portion of the Kabbalah however it's not the first book concerning the Kabbalah unlike that of Sefer ha-Bahir or Book of Brightness from the 12th century.

However, the Zohar is regarded among the most popular works on Kabbalah We are grateful to Gershom Scholem Gershom Scholem, an Israeli philosopher who was born in Germany. We should also acknowledge those who translated Zohar in English. Zohar with the

Zohar in English. Although the Zohar is difficult to comprehend even when translated, because of the text's complex, cryptic theology, it can be explored which is where you will find an entire world of imagination and many things to consider spiritually in order to gain insights.

* The Zohar's author. Zohar

Moses witnessed the Zohar at Mount Sinai. The Zohar was revealed to Moses by God himself. He then passed it to him by word of mouthuntil Rabbi Shimon bar-Yochai wrote the text in the second century, though the issue of who wrote it is still a subject of debate.

Researchers believe that the Zohar was written in the 13th century of Spain in Spain by Rabbi Moshe de Leon and perhaps other writers. The text has been written in Aramaic which was not utilized in the time of the Zohar. It is possible that the writer decided to use this language to make the text appear more ancient than it actually is. However, De Leon credits Rabbi Shimon who was a secluded cave for more than 10 years studying the Torah.

The source of this book is questionable since it was discovered by a single individual and speaks about events that occurred in the Talmudic period, while also claiming to be older than. There's also an account of the widow of de Leon who was given money to purchase the original manuscript, but admitted that he had only claimed"the" Zohar had been Rabbi Shimon's work in order to enhance its value. Some critics believe that they believe she may have earned some money by selling the manuscript , but she was not convinced that it was worthwhile and thus she made up to claim that she was husband's the true writer. It's an unsubstantiated claim, that hasn't stopped the spreading of the novel.

* The main thrusts of the Zohar

The Zohar discusses the cosmos and its real nature. It discusses God's essence as well as the Creation the way in which Ein Sof and Sephirot are interconnected and the significance of evil and sin as well as the Torah as well as sacred days, rituals and much more.

The book explains that words and numbers are powerful and are the reason we created the universe. Language draws strength from our speech on earth, by which we can create change both on the earth and in other realms by prayers and contemplation, and divine speech that creates and recreates the world every single day, forever.

A large portion of Zohar is in sermons as well as commentary, all of which are in accordance with the Torah's books. holy Torah. It is an revelatory of the more profound, hidden meanings of the text found in the Torah. The entire collection of Bible tales and characters are considered as belonging to the Divine and as metaphors for the soul's various levels. The Zohar also addresses the issue that is the 10 Sephirot that we've covered.

The Zohar is a must-read text to read for the Kabbalist that is on the road towards spiritual awakening. In the Zohar studying is the most moral and religious act that is sure to connect you the connection to Ein Sof and help you reach enlightenment.

Zohar Zohar was written in the rather obscure and cryptic style Aramaic that was the main language that was spoken during the Second Temple, from 539 BCE until 70 CE. It was the original language used in many of the works from Ezra or Daniel and is the main dialect used throughout the Talmud. Aramaic was also used by Jews at the end of the second half in the Middle Ages. There are some scholars who believe it is possible that Zohar was composed by someone who wasn't an indigenous speaker of the Aramaic language, since there were Galician-Portuguese words and Andalusi Romance included in the text.

God's union with God

Kabbalah seeks to bring about the connection between humans with the Divine through ceremonies and study. In the pages, Zohar describe the process of contemplation by using a person who is erotic. Mystics tend to study in the late hours of the night, so the relationship to mystics and the Divine and mystic can be considered to be a relationship that is shared by two lovebirds. This is because God or Shekinah is the bride. studying, prayer, and meditation all resemble spiritual union with the Divine in which the mystic can lose himself in the Divine. This is known as devekut and is a form of devotion to God. The Zohar makes use of the concept of unity in the sex and birth to describe this process that occurs in both divine and the human.

The Zohar is an influential text for both Jews as well as non-Jews. The Zohar was written by Ti. Zohar that paved the way for the development of the other Kabbalistic texts such as those of Rabbi Isaac Luria. The Zohar is also a text that Christian scholars have begun to accept. They have noticed the similarities that exist between the cosmological system, as well as in specific aspects of Christian theology such as the notion that The Holy Trinity. The influence of the Zohar became more prominent due to Hasidism, a religion where Kabbalistic concepts became more refined into psychological theories.

Reading the Zohar

Many of the traditional teachings suggest waiting until 40 before studying Kabbalah so that you're mentally and spiritually prepared to study these texts. The texts are complex, dense, and complex, making them an excellent study for those who are interested in more deeply into the Jewish texts. You'll require the fundamental knowledge in Torah, Talmud, Midrash, Aramaic, and Hebrew. New translations are available to help make the Zohar an easier to read, however the complex nature of the huge imagined setting of the Zohar can make it difficult to study without the fundamental knowledge or advice of a scholar who will help you navigate the challenging portions.

* Acceptance to The Zohar in Judaism

The most commonly accepted belief is that God revealed the Kabbalistic doctrines to great Biblical characters such as Moses as well as Abraham. Then , these teachings were transmitted through oral tradition through the Biblical times until they were removed in the time of Shimon Bar Yochai. But, according to contemporary researchers, such as Gersgom Scholem who has looked into the Zohar and found it possible that the original author is Moses de Leon. There's also a possibility that an earlier text in the Zohar was written before the time of Leon and the other text was added slowly.

There are other Orthodox groups and non-Chasidic Orthodox groups and even non-Orthodox Jews religions that consider in the Zohar is not more than a pseudepigrapha. The works have been incorrectly attributable to the wrong writer or work that the original author credits to an old source or figure. Some people believe they believe that Zohar belongs to Apocrypha meaning obscure, secret writings that were intended to be only studied by the members of a particular group. Some believe in this but are still comfortable taking meaning through the words of Zohar while recognizing its teachings as suitable for Judaism in the present.

The adherents to Dor Deah are devoted to the Dor Deah movement do not believe in the

Zohar. Portuguese as well as Spanish Jews got rid of all references to the Zohar in their liturgy as well as siddyrs shortly after Sabbatai Zevi was ordained as a Rabbi from Smyrna was a convert to Judaism and embraced Islam. There are elements of the Zohar which have been added back into Portuguese siddurim, as well as Spanish siddurim. This is even true for those who haven't restored those elements from the Zohar in their liturgy. Therefore the siddurim which editors who are not Orthodox Jews may contain elements from the Zohar and other works regardless of the fact that those who are responsible for editing don't believe they're an oral tradition that dates back to Moses The time of Moses.

*The Zohar outside of Judaism

There are those who follow different religions, or do not adhere to any particular religion, but are interested in the Zohar in the interest of curiosity or because they are seeking real and relevant answers to the most fundamental questions concerning the meaning of existence and living the reason for this existence and what the nature's laws are, and how we fit in the context of these laws as well as other issues that can keep our souls occupied and keep us awake all midnight.

According to the conventional rabbinic Judaism view as well as the Zohar itself the main purpose is to help the Jews throughout the process of Exile and shed illumination on the wisdom of Torah and mitzvot. Torah and mitzvot as well as Judaic laws.

* Criticisms of Zohar Zohar

It was in 1851 that Adolf Jellinek began the sequence of systematic and academic criticism of the Zohar's authorship Zohar through the publication of his monograph Moses ben Shem-tob de Leon und sein Verhaltnis to Sohar at the time of 1851. The subject was later taken up by Heinrich Graetz, a young historian, who published it in History of the Jews, volume 7.

After many years of thorough study, Scholem pointed out in 1941 that de Leon had to be the writer, and he also observed that the writer was guilty of a number of mistakes in his Aramaic and had also added Spanish sentences and phrases which clearly indicated that the writer had very little understanding of Israel.

Many experts think that the Zohar was composed by a group, and not only de Leon. They believe that de Leon led a mystical school, and that this school is the one responsible for the Zohar. Although de Leon may have indeed composed the text, its content isn't fake. A few parts may be based upon the traditional text and it was common practice to attribute credit to the older Rabbis, so the text would be more important. It's possible de Leon assumed the position as a channel for the sake of Rabbi Shimon bar Yochai.

Professor Gershom Scholem wrote an essay published in Encyclopaedia Judaica where he provided a thorough analysis of all Zohar's referenced sources. Scholem believes that the author was using a variety of Jewish sources that existed. However Scholem created a good amount of fictional text such as the Sifra de-Hanokh as well as the Sifra-de-Adam and The Sifra de-Rav Hamnuna Sava as well as the Sifra de-Shelomo Malka and the Sifra de-Aggadeta and the Sifra de-Rav Yeiva Sava, the Raza de-Razin and many more. The majority of Kabbalistic historians agree that Scholem's ideas are correct, however, there are some who question whether he's correct.

The majority of the concepts that are contained in Zohar have their roots in fictional works, however, a number of older and rabbinic mystical notions are presented, with no source being mentioned. The vast majority of concepts in the Zohar originate from the Talmud as well as other midrash books as well as Jewish mythological works from earlier times.

According to Scholem that The writer had a deep understanding in the material that he had previously referenced and utilized to build his writings. He was able to create his personal variations, based on sources from the Babylonian Talmud for most of his sources, as well as his own sources, including the Midrash Tanhuma, the Midrash Rabbah as well as each Pesiktot (the Pesikta Rabbati or Pesikta De-Rav Kahana). He also made reference to his Pirkei de-Rabbi Eliezer as well as his Midrash regarding the Psalms as well as the Targum Onkelos. He doesn't cite them exactly however, he translates the texts into his own unique style.

De Leon also didn't refer too much to the halakhic Midrashim or in the Jerusalem Talmud, or the other Targums. There isn't much mention of the Aggadah Shir ha-Shirim and The Alfabet de-Rav Akiva as well as the Midrash on Proverbs. It's unclear if the author was referring to Yalkut Shimoni or were they aware of the sources for the aggadah on their own. He did mention the smaller Midrashim, such as those of the Alfabet de-Ben Sira, the Hekhalot Rabbati and the Baraita de-Ma'aseh Bereshit and the Sefer Zerubbabel and many more.

Sefer ha Bahir

The Sefer ha Bahir is also known as The Book of Illumination or the Book of Brightness. The work is considered to be mysterious and anonymous. It's usually believed to be the work of the rabbinic sage, Nehunya ben HaKanah, in the 1st century and also a possible contemporaneous of Jewish Rabbi Yochanan ben Zakai. The reason this is the case is the fact that this Sefer ha Bahir begins with the words "R. Nehunya ben HaKanah stated." "The Book of Brightness is also known as The Midrash that Rabbi Nehunya was a part of HaKanah. It is an early study on the esoteric facets of Judaism that was later called Kabbalah.

Moses ben Nahman, also known as Nachmanides, or Ramban (or Bonastruc ca Porta) was a medieval Jewish scholar with a reputation as a physician, a Sephardic Rabbi as well as the Kabbalist scholar also a Biblical commentator. He was among the first to quote the work of the Book of Lightness under the title Midrash R. Nehunya ben HaKanah as a commentary to the Torah. Medieval Kabbalists refer to the work as Sefer HaBahir due to the first statement it makes. That comment is: "And now men see the darkness that is shining (bahir) on the sky. (Job Chapter 27, verse 21,).

The authorship for Sefer ha Bahir Sefer ha Bahir

According to Kabbalists that the source for this book Sefer ha Bahir belongs to the Rabbi Nehunya of the Mishnaic period, which was around 100 CE. Medieval Kabbalists believed they believed that Sefer ha Bahir was not an unified book. Instead, they read fragments scattered across scrolls and booklets. Because of its fragmented nature, it is likely that certain discussions take place the middle of a sentence and the book shifts from one subject to the next, which makes it possible that it was written broken up before it was put together in a complete form.

The study of history shows that the book was written in a later time. In the past, scholars believed the book was composed through Isaac the Blind the French Rabbi with a wealth of written works about Kabbalah and was alive in the 13th century. If he did not compose it, they argue then it could have been composed by students of his school. The line, "And now men see not the light that is bright in the sky," is rather on its own and not interconnected with the rest that follows. The author was simply referring to the author's blindness.

However, more modern Kabbalistic experts believe that at least one portions in the Sefer ha Bahir must have been adapted from an older work, specifically that of the Sefer the Raza Rabba. In this earlier work there are references of the Geonim as well as their works. But, there's no fully-fledged copy of Sefer Raza Rabba anywhere in existence. There are quotations from the book in earlier works. Ronit Meroz, a scholar claims it is believed that the Book of Illumination elements goes back to Babylonia which was around the 10th century. Meroz cites the Babylonian vowel points system that was eventually discarded and many other evidence that suggests the book was probably written in Provence during the 12th century.

A number of Kabbalistic experts think it is possible that Sefer ha Bahir has elements of Gnosticism to the earlier works that it quotes. Therefore, the question of what extent Gnosticism has had an impact on Kabbalah is a matter of investigation. It is possible to look into the work by Moshe Idel as well as Gershom Scholem to find out more about this.

The story of the Sefer ha Bahir

Kabbalists claim it's possible that Illumination's oral heritage extends far back to the 1st century CE. They believe it's impossible to exclude the possibility that these manuscripts were already in use prior to the time they were released during the period of 12th century. The Provence Kabbalists' school issued their work, the Sefer ha Bahir, and they distributed the text to a small public in the form of an unpublished manuscript in the year 1174. In 1298, the manuscript was the first, and only remaining manuscript, dating to the latter half of the 13th century.

In 1331, the first commentaries on the holy text was written by a pupil from the legendary Rashba of Shlomo ben Aderet. Rabbi Meir ben Shalom Abi-Sahula. This Sefer ha Bahir was then unannouncedly published under the name Or HaGanuz. In the late 15th century it was known that the Sefer ha Bahir had been translated by

Flavius Mithridates into Latin. Unfortunately, the translation was to be too long and useless.

161 was the year 161 was when the Bahir was released along with The Mayan HaChakhmah in Amsterdam, in the form of a book. In 1706, The Book of Brightness was also released along with the Mayan HaChakhmah in Berlin. Since then, it's also been printed by Sklav, Koretz, Lvov, Vilna, and Jerusalem. It was also published in a location unidentified, as element of Chamisha Chumshei Kabbalah. Gershom Scholem himself wrote an original German version of Sefer ha Bahir in 1923. In 1979 Rabbi Aryeh Kaplan published the English translation. In the year following, Fracois Secret published the Latin translation. At the time of the 1995 edition the Hebrew text was available in Daniel Abrams' manuscripts. 2005 saw the publication of the Latin Sefer ha Bahir by Flavius Mithridates and the edition of Saverio Campanini.

Rabbi Isaac HaKohen, a Kabbalist from the 13th century stated that Sefer ha Bahir is "from the region from Israel to the first pietists, the sages of Ashkenaz and the Kabbalists from Germany.

Then, the book traveled to the wise men of the beginning in Provence who pursue various recorded (records that are of) wisdom, and those who possess the ultimate, supernatural wisdom. However, they only saw a portion of the book , and not all of it since they could not view the entire book in its totality."

In the Book of Illumination, you can discover a number of literary layers. Certain of them were written toward the close of the 9th century, in the East. Some were written as early as the 10th century, while others were written were written in Provence during the middle of the century.

The Book utilizes the Babylonian Grammar and vocalization system that result in a distinct pronunciation that was extremely popular throughout the East. This is the very fact that indicates that there is an Oriental aspect to the text. While we have the Tiberian vocalization in Hebrew however, the Babylonian vocalization is predominantly higher (with marks over each letter). It also has it's segol (a Hebraic vowel sign composed of three dots that make an upside-down triangular in a sort of) that is pronounced the same way as the patah (another Hebraic vowel sign represented by a horizontal line below the letter). Should it were true that the Book of Brightness were written in a place that utilized the Babylonian system and the assertion that the Divine placed the patah above the letter, and an segol underneath would have more significance.

In the vocalization system used in Babylon the patah vowel is considered to be higher, in contrast, segol is considered lower. segol can be lower within the Tiberian system. Thus it is the only system that Babylonian vocalization system permits users to pronounce the two sets of vowels in one go since they are both pronounce in the same manner.

It is believed that the Babylonian vocalization system utilized to represent the Holy is the reason for the writing the text. In the beginning in the 10th century there was a tense debate about what grammatical system was the most appropriate one to depict the Torah in Jewish communities. The Tiberian system prevailed, but all agreed they were all aware that Babylonian system had a different influence on the traditional Hebrew. The Babylonian system was no longer an instrument for symbolizing the Holy. Babylonian was written before the Tiberian one. Babylonian Layer was made ahead of the Tiberian one gained.

* The contents from Sefer ha Bahir. Sefer ha Bahir

The Book of Illumination is in the form of an exegetical based midrash that is based in the Bible of Genesis specifically, the first chapter. It is divided into short paragraphs, which are 60 in total 140 pages, and is written in the form of dialogue, in a dialogue between followers and the master.

The main characters of the book include Rabbi Rahamai or Rehumai, and Rabbi Amora or Amorai. Certain statements are found in the holy book that are attributed to Rabbi Johanan, Rabbi Berechiah and Rabbi Bun Rabbi Bun, who later were mentioned within Midrashic literature.

The Sefer ha Bahir has several commentary that provide insight into the Bible verses and their mystic significance. It also reveals the mystical significance of the Hebrew letters, their shapes, vowel marks, some of the assertions in the Sefer Yetzirah or the Book of Creation and the ways in which sacred names are utilized in the realm of magic.

There 200 paragraphs. It's similar to aphorisms found in The Book of Illumination. Each paragraph is a reference to the Torah for a better understanding of its meanings. Similar to other texts from the Kabbalah The meanings of these passages are based on many symbolic meanings and are open to a variety of interpretations.

The analogy is constant throughout the book, in which the queen, a king as well as his gardens along with his servants and garden are utilized to convey the meaning of the book. Each paragraph contains a reference to other sections in different ways and can be broken the sections into five parts because of Aryeh Kaplan's interpretation. You can group them but not necessarily in a strict manner. They remain within the same themes.

• Sections from the Sefer ha Bahir

1. Section (verses 1-16) It contains all the commentary on the first passages from the Creation story from Genesis. Genesis.

2. (verses 17 through 44) The information in this section is regarding the Hebrew alphabet, or the Aleph-Beth as well as uses an ancient text called the Sefer Yetzirah, which demonstrates how these letters are linked to the mysticism that is found throughout the Torah.

3. (verses 45-122) This is about The Sephirot along with the Seven voices.

4. (verses between 124 and 193) It is about the 10 Sephirot

The 5th section (verses 193-200) The conclusion of this section is the entire dialogue. It is also known by the title "Mysteries of the Soul."

Sefer ha Bahir Sefer ha Bahir is the book which discusses the Sephirot according to Kabbalah as divine powers and attributes that originate from the One.

*The Creation of the World

As per the Book of Brightness, the world doesn't result from an act of creativity. As with the Divine Book of Brightness, the book exists throughout time and not only in terms of possibility. It is said that the Sefer ha Bahir teaches that the universe was created out of the simplest manifestation of the hidden HaGanuz which is the name of the original Sephirah which is also called Keter Elyon, which is an expression of God.

The Sephirah created Hokmah (or the wisdom) and, from it, Binah (or intelligence) was born. From these three called the superior Sephirot and from the primary principles of the universe the seven lesser Sephirot emerged. From them were born the universe with all its physicality.

Each Sephirot is connected to one another and all of them have characteristics that are both passive and active which means they both emit and receive. The movement between to the next Sephirah from one to another one can be portrayed through one of the Hebrew letter that make up the alphabet. Thus, the letter gimel that is made of a tube that has both ends opened is the symbol of the letter Sephirah. On one side, it gets strength, and at the other end it releases it. Imagine Sephirot as God's energy as well as the different manifestations that God appears.

* Reincarnation according to the Sefer ha Bahir

It is believed that the Sefer ha Bahir answers the question of why people who are good suffer through horrible experiences while bad people perform exceptionally well, by introducing the idea of Reincarnation. It states that people who are successful currently were bad in their previous lives, and the wicked simply in their past lives.

Gilgul, also known as the soul's transmigration, metempsychosis or reincarnation was not accepted by Jewish philosophy, but in Kabbalah the concept is taken as a given. It is said that the Sefer Bahir has explained this concept in many parables. And since there was no justification in the matter, it's evident that this was an idea that was developed and spread in the early Kabbalists and had no specific connection to transmigration. It is stated in Ecclesiastes chapter 1 chapter 1, verse 4 "One generation goes away and another one comes." It is presumed that the generation that dies is the same generation that will take its place.

These parables, as well as the Aggadah in the Talmud were explained in transmigratory terminology. It's unclear whether there was a connection between the emergence of metempsychosis, a Kabbalistic belief system that made the rounds throughout the south of France and then its evolution in the Cathars of the present who lived a healthy life. They considered that the soul had to transfer to the body of an animal, whereas it is the case that Sefer ha Bahir only mentions this notion about the human body.

Following the publication of the Book of Illumination, the Gilgul concept was developed various directions before becoming one of the primary theories of Kabbalah although Kabbalists themselves differ regarding the exact details of the whole. At the time of the 13th century Gilgul was considered as esoteric, and was never mentioned. In the 14th century arrived it was awash with a variety of explicit instructions on the subject. In the context of philosophy, the word ha'atakah, or "transference" was used to refer to Gilgul. Within Kabbalistic literature, you'll only hear the word gilgul appear in the text from the Sefer ha Temunah and others following. The followers of Isaac the Blind along with the Gerona Kabbalists, often discuss the secrets of impregnation or labor. It was in the 14th century when the terms gilgul and ibbur became separated. In the time that of Zohar and up to the present, gilgul became a very popular word in Hebrew writings and works of philosophy.

There are Bible commands and passages that are that are translated into the word gilgul. Certain earlier sects believed in the ritual slaughter laws or shechita as proof of the Bible that transmigration was an event. This was in accordance with their beliefs about transmigration between animals. The Kabbalists break away from these sects, and instead turn to the law of levirate marriage to prove for the gilgul doctrine. (The Levirate wedding is the custom where one's brother who is without children at the time of his death becomes the husband and grants himself children, at the following gilgul). In later times, some mitzvot were understood by the gilgul. Gilgul also explains the apparent injustice in the world.

The story of Job and the mystery behind the story were examined by gilgul as a lens. The earlier Kabbalists and even the Zohar's writer did not see transmigration as something that was universally applicable, impacting all living things (not like the Indians consider it to be) They did not think of transmigration as something applicable to all human beings.

Instead, they saw it as a consequence of violations committed against the natural process of procreation, as well as transgressions of sexual nature.

Gilgul is considered to be punishment and is a brutal one indeed for those who have to undergo it. In the same way, it demonstrates God's mercy. God since there is no one who is banished to be a void forever. Even those who are destined to lose their souls or die (keritut) have an opportunity to improve by the gilgul. A few put too much attention on the fairness that comes with transmigration. Others are more focused on mercy. The purpose of transmigration is to cleanse the soul and give it a possibility to begin over again and improve. One way to ensure that your previous mistakes are punished in this perspective also involves deaths of babies.

According to the Sefer ha Bahir states that Reincarnations can last for many generations However in accordance with Spanish Kabbalah, for one to be able to repent to their transgressions their soul must go through three times more transmigration following the first time it enters its body. This is in accordance with Job Chapter 33. Verse 29, Behold, God, does all the above, three times, twice in the presence of a man. But, righteous souls will reincarnate repeatedly, but to benefit the world, and not for their own benefits. There are various opinions regarding the perpetual resurrection of the righteous from Kabbalistic writings, for instance, there is the belief that states that the righteous cross over three times, while the unrighteous will transmigrate for the sake of a thousand.

Funerals must be held before a new gilgul is able to occur so the burial needs to be conducted within the same day as the deceased person dies. Sometimes an individual soul of a male incarnates as a female, and this causes the sterility. Souls that transmigrate into the female bodies of both women and gentiles was thought to be a possibility by many Kabbalists. This view is which is completely different from those who follow Safed Kabbalah. According to the Sefer Peli'ah sees all proselytes as Jewish souls who passed into the bodies of gentiles and returned to their original state.

There's a lot to disagreement about the concept of reincarnation and hell. Bahya ben Asher claims that transmigration occurs only after one has accepted their fate in the eternal hellfire, but the contrary view can be mentioned in the Zohar as well as within the Ra'aya Mehemna and even among the vast majority of Kabbalists. The fact that hell and gilgul are inextricably linked, which means that there is no compromise that can be found between both. As per Joseph of Hamadan from Persia Hell is transmigration between animals.

Some believe that souls started transmigrating following the time that Abel was killed, while others believe that this occurred in the time of the generation who was a part of the Flood The transmigration process will come to an end after the deceased are revived. Then the bodies of all who were reincarnated will return to life along with their Nizot (or sparks) that came from their souls inside them will be spread.

Reincarnation was a concept that was developed as a punishment that was confined to certain sins to an overall concept caused the rise of the idea of transmigration to animals, plans, and other nonliving things. However, a lot of Kabbalists were fiercely against this notion but it wasn't picked up in until after 1400.

The first reference to the idea of reincarnation in animals' bodies was found in the Sefer ha-Temunah, which has its roots within a circle who were part of The Gerona Kabbalists. There isn't any mention of this notion in the Zohar however there are some passages are found inside the Tikkunei Zohar which attempt to make this concept clear and implying that this belief was already well-known for the author of this work.

There's an anonymous book about the meaning of the commandments, referred to by the name of Ta'amei ha-Mitzvot, published around 1290 - 1300. It includes a number of specifics regarding the transformation from the soul of a human into the animal body and, in all those details, it appears the transmigration took place due to engaging in sexual activities that the Torah explicitly prohibits.

For more details on the concept of gilgul it is possible to look at studies by Joseph bar Shalom Ashkenazi and his knowledgeable colleagues who were born around the time of the 14th century. They believe that transmigration occurs in all forms of existence including the Sephiro to angels and even nonliving objects. They refer to this as din benei Halof or sod ha-shelah.

In accordance with this Kabbalistic perspective everything around us are in the change of their forms. They fall to their lowest state, and then rise again to their most pristine form. This is why the extremely logical concept of reincarnation the soul to another is completely obscured. In its placeis the law of the change of the form.

Perhaps it is best to consider this interpretation of gilgul as a solution to the constant philosophical question that stems from the definition that the soul is the body's shape that is unable to change into another body's body as per Aristotle. The Safed Kabbalists support the concept of gilgul in which one soul can transmute to all forms in the natural world. It is because of those Safed Kabbalists that this view was popularized.

* Commentaries and editions from Sefer ha Bahir. Sefer ha Bahir

The most precise of the Sefer ha Bahir's writings, in its current form is the one composed by Meir ben Solomon Abi-Sahula around 1331. He had published his comments about The Sefer ha Bahir, Or HaGanuz which translates to "The The Hidden Light" in secret. Since then his commentary on the Sefer ha Bahir was translated into German and English by Gershom Scholem and Aryeh Kaplan and Aryeh Kaplan, respectively. More recently Saverio Campanini has offered an even more thorough edit, which proves extremely valuable.

Chapter 5: Kabbalah As A Spiritual Practice

Although the Kabbalah is millennia old it is is still being studied by both Jews as well as non-Jews. It is frequently being studied in conjunction with yoga, meditation as well as other spiritual practices. It is frequently followed by those who pursue the path of a fairy-tale to attain enlightenment.

Many people, when they learn about the Kabbalah they would like to be aware than just the meanings of words, or Peshat however, but also the deeper meanings that can lead to greater spiritual understanding.

We are only aware of a tiny part of what's around us at any given time this is the thing that the Kabbalah is teaching us. Our minds naturally block out the majority of the world around us since there's just an overwhelming amount of sensory input and we'd be overwhelmed. There's so much information available that our brains have developed the capability to, as a survival strategy to disregard what it perceives (often at an unconscious level) as non-important.

Consider it for an instant You are thinking about buying an Mercedes C class car because there aren't many of them in the streets So you browse advertisements and consider having one. Then you realize that they are everywhere and it appears that everyone owns these cars! Are these cars in existence before you decided to buy one? They existed and existed however your mind was not able to see them because they didn't matter to you.

As you will see, it's easy to realize that there is more to life than only what you perceive, but the issue is how, if are interested in it, can you see more and feel more enjoyment and connection to those things that matter to you? This is the goal when you receive Kabbalah, i.e., you will experience more of the world through an understanding that is deeper.

The most commonly used method to connect with the universe and all the things around them is by using practices of meditation. If you can slow down the speed of thought that is your mind and be more aware of your thoughts with greater clarity and see what you see in greater in detail.

from a psychological point perspective, those who meditate are more attuned to how they feel and think about. They can notice negative emotions they are able to pick up and manage these before they can take over and create problems. Meditation can provide numerous physical benefits, which have all been proved scientifically.

When you are meditating you'll find that you feel more calm and less prone to feel emotions. With meditation, you will be able to observe everything around you more clearly and with greater depth.

The ancient form of meditation was not practiced with Kabbalah up until around the turn of the century. However, the majority of teachers today combine Kabbalah along with meditation.

The Theosophical movement of the Victorian time period accepted Kabbalah with full acceptance, recognizing its long history as well as the fact the fact that it was an ideal system to help map out the entire universe as well as various things within it.

The ten sefirot in the Kabbalistic tree can be experienced on many different levels: emotional spiritual, intellectual, and physical. You have the option of taking time to integrate each sefirah in your daily life on all level. levels.As you master every aspect of each sefirah, you'll become more spiritual and gain greater understanding of this mysterious system.

If you intend to be a serious learner of the Kabbalah and the Zohar, you'll have to be familiar with the Zohar. The book is full of wisdom regarding the Kabbalah and will assist anyone seeking to develop spiritually and develop. If you read the Zohar together with the Kabbalah it will be evident that you become more spiritual and are increasingly aware of mysteries in it.

Keep in mind that if you want to really comprehend the Kabbalah and utilize it for anything, even spiritual development You will need to master at least the basics of Hebrew language. While you don't have to be proficient of the dialect, being able to comprehend the meaning of the most important words spoken in the native language can help you grow and improve your comprehension of each sefirah.

There are many options to think about the Kabbalah. The one you pick is your choice, and you can choose to focus on one for a period of time until you've mastered the concept, or change between them as you feel comfortable. The latter is the most effective method since you'll see the most results faster.

The most well-known methods of meditation is to focus about the words of God. It is possible to use them as mantras, and then work through different combinations of letters. Each combination will possess its own characteristics and abilities that you are able to be able to comprehend and grasp. While there many names that have been attributed to Kabbalists

You can begin with the gods of God and then work your way up from there.

Mandalas can be used (a form or pattern) which is a wonderful method to sit and contemplate. It could be the complete tree of life, or just some of it. You could utilize Hebrew words or letters as mandalas in your meditation.

A different form of meditation is known as Yihudim, the practice of bringing together opposing forces, e.g., male and female or heaven and earth etc. This type of meditation seeks to dispel the illusion of separating physical reality and the spiritual. One of the objectives when studying Kabbalah is to bring together your body, mind, and spirit with the Light.

It is also possible to meditate through achieving inner quiet and looking into the Light while you are open to receiving wisdom and direction. If you can connect this way the divine wisdom will flow into you and inspire you.

One of the most popular ways to meditate is to connect with your Ain which is the eternal via the inner silence. Invoking the Ain will assist you in defeating and release the negative energy that is a part of everyone of us. It can help you free yourself out of ego and reduce the inner noise that keeps us from our spiritual practice. If there is a state called Ain it means that you have a position where you are free to do whatever you want and you are open to receiving the divine wisdom and understanding.

Prayer is another type practice of mindfulness that's very popular and simple to practice. It is possible to recite prayers, texts from the holy scriptures or simply be yourself and speak to God. When you are open and talking to Him and allowing Him to speak to you, you will be able to ease the stress you feel and break down the barriers between yourself and God the Source. You can do this at any moment you like regardless of whether it's in a holy spot such as your car, or sitting on an outdoor bench.

You may also contemplate every sefirah. Beginning at the bottom of the sefirah the sefirah, you will work through all the elements of each sefirah and develop an understanding that is thorough and profound of them prior to moving towards the following. When you incorporate every sefirah into your daily life and begin to follow the principles that it teaches you will develop an comprehension of Kabbalah as well as each of the 10 sefirot. This is a process which can take years since each sefirah can be an in-depth subject that has numerous aspects and a lot to be learned about it.

The way you practice meditation and incorporate the Kabbalah within your spiritual practices is entirely up to you and the process will differ for everyone based on their backgrounds and motivations to study the Kabbalah. Choose the approach you feel comfortable with and that work for you.

Chapter 6: All You Need To Learn About The History Of Fortune Telling

The very idea of the origins of playing cards has been obscured in the mists time.

The first recorded evidence of tarot cards was found in northern Italy in the 16th century.

It was believed that Tarot cards were a product of the past in Egypt and were brought to Europe by Gypsies. But, there isn't any strong proof to back this belief.

The first recorded mention of tarot decks comes via Martiano da Tortona, who wrote about them in 1425, while being imprisoned for heresy. Tarot cards were popular throughout Europe from the beginning of time. They were developed during the Tang Dynasty in China at the time of the Tang Dynasty and spread to Europe in the 14th century.

In 1436, the card game began to spread across northwestern Italy through France before spreading to Spain around 1450.

The term "triumphs" began to be utilized in 1440 to describe a poker-like game played by four players.

It was the first deck of tarot that has been created by Filippo Maria Visconti, in 1441, for the mother of his son, Bianca Maria Visconti, the third wife of Duke Filippo Maria of Milan.

The first decks that were used for playing cards date to the 15th century. They were found in England, France and Italy.

Cartomancy was a well-known method for divination within Germany from 1410 onwards; the first recorded German deck dates to 1435.

There are some scholars who believe they came to Europe around the Middle Ages as a result of trade with Arabs who took their culture from Indians and who then acquired them through the Chinese.

The first evidence of that existence of card originates from China in the Tang Dynasty, and they were most likely used for divination. They were adorned with symbols from the Iching, the renowned Book of Changes, and the Ideogram that was associated with it.

A late , unofficial text states that, around 1120, a court official gave thirty-two ivory tablets in exchange for a gift to the emperor.

Certain of them dealt with natural elements, like the earth and sky as well as human beings, but they all were about fate or abstract guidelines to follow in order to be a decent citizen.

The Emperor had them reproduced and they spread throughout his empire. I

The game known as A Thousand Times Ten Thousand was played with only thirty cards, three sets of nine cards each , and three arcanas or victories.

They therefore had"three "seeds."

* Jian or Qian (coins),

* Tiao

(strings made of coin, in which they are referred to as string because of the hole Chinese coins have to hang and the stacking of the coins on strings),

* Wan (ten thousand),

*, and then added three additional single cards: Qian Wan (Thousand Times Ten Thousand), Hong Hua (Red Flower) and Bai Hua (White Flower).

These were depicted as Ideograms that had numbers between 2 and 9 , on each of the 3 seeds.

There are some scholars who suggest that the initial cards actually represented real money that served as being used as a tool to play and a wager.

On the cards , there were four red symbols that represented the cardinal virtues of kindness, justice, order and wisdom - each one of which was depicted four times.

The sum of all the symbols during the game added in the amount of stars which is an entire microcosm.

In China the cards travelled or evolved simultaneously to India which is the birthplace of chess.

From the Indians The Arabs took them in and, in the 14th century, via Spain and south Italy they brought them throughout Europe.

These Arab cards, also known as Haib they were, in reality, only numerical or symbolic, due to the prohibition in the Koran to duplicate human figures. The ones of the Europeans who did never and could not have adhered to these prohibitions, were immediately enriched by various images and, at times, bizarre shapes.

The first decks of cards found in the West were very similar to Chinese symbols, providing an ethical and civic lesson, and transforming the microcosm's order to the larger order of the universe.

Naibi, or the Naibi are a part of the Arabic Haib which was a popular name in Italy during the 14th century, were a sort of reminder of moral and civil rules to be observed and consisted of fifty pictures, divided into five sets of 10 cards.

The series was related to:

The conditions of life, starting from the most humble, to the most awe-inspiring physical and spiritual power (the beggar and the servant, merchant, the craftsman the knight, the lord, the scholar and the king pope and the emperor) and the nine Muses, to which Apollo was added to the Sciences by using cards that symbolize the planets and in the realm of Virtues.

It was basically an educational game and was augmented with the numbers of the cards. The latter could have been was inspired by dice (Ace Two, Three etc.) and the characters could have been influenced from the game of chess. King Queen, King, Knight.

The oldest known deck of cards dates back to Venice which was in use in the fourteenth century. It consists of 78 cards that are divided by two types.

The first set includes 22 cards referred to Tarot cards. They are symbolic compositions, likely intended for education reasons, and thus directly derived of the Naibi.

The second section contains 56 cards that are divided into four series , color suits comprising 14 cards: clubs , rods, cups, swords as well as Coinsor Denarii.

According to Wirth an extremely well-known and well-known tarot scholars the symbolism that is associated with the suit of cards relates to the occult and corresponds to a mystical quaternary.

According to this interpretation, the possession of four instruments - the scepter the cup the sword, money - confers the status of a skilled or an occult master.

For the initiators, the meaning of the cards represented an alphanumeric code in which certain combinations could provide an explanation of destiny.

The concepts contained inside the Tarot are timeless and unchangeable.

They are a result of the very first demands of the observer who was afflicted by the desire to provide an appearance, a shape, or a number as a symbol of his amazing fantasies about the universe's mechanism.

Cartomancy and occultism entered smaller circles in the middle of the Middle Ages, without causing either scandal or surprise.

But, the actual research into cards did not begin until 1500 in the year 1500, when Guillaume de Postel, a mathematician, philosopher , and orientalist wrote his first book, The Key to Occult Things and began an period of study on cards.

According to Postel The word "Tarot" originates of"the Egyptian "Taro," which was a reference to "royal road" or "road of the kings" He also stated it was possible that the Tarot "game" is inspired by the Egyptian game called Tari.

Furthermore it also was Postel himself who spotted the link between the cards and the Kabbalah and the primary components and seeds.

The era of theory.

From the late 17th century and the beginning of the part of the century that followed The spiritualist and magician Emanuel Swedenborg worked in Sweden and Norway.

He was a renowned scholar of Kabbalah and occultism, esotericism and hypnosis. He was revered by Balzac as well as Emanuel Kant himself.

The first the esoteric game was created that limited itself to the world of the cards and which mostly focused on the many great destiny of man and a fervent returning to instigatory knowledge, which is a common phrase from"the "century of limes".

At the turn of the century,, there was a huge spread of occult style and a large game of divination started to flourish.

With the help of Court de Gebelin (1725-1784) and his illustrious followers Alliette who was a French hairdresser whose name is his anagram Etteilla cartomancy was given an important increase.

Advocates of the Egyptian roots of tarot they tried to turn divination as a technique into an actual science.

Etteilla, in particular, said she believed that Tarot was first created at the time of the year 2170 B.C., during a gathering of Egyptian magicians, which was presided over by Hermes Trismegistus. Then as time passed the characters of the Tarot have lost their original features.

Etteilla was then able to create an entirely new Tarot deck, called the Great Etteilla or Book of Toth that, though acknowledged as fake, eventually became an integral part of the cartomancy tradition. I

in a collection of tiny volumes that were published between 1783 and 1785. Etteilla said that his Tarot deck is a mystical guide for examining the future.

He was an opportunist with a keen eye and had a captivating personality capable of changing people's minds. In order to ensure that his ideas were fully successful, he created the Society of

Interpreters of the Book of Toth, through which the theories of the book became popular throughout Europe.

Since then cartomancy that was practiced widely throughout Italy as well as France for more than two centuries, was a fashion.

Even through the French Revolution, the divinatory passion did not decrease however there was changes in the depiction of the characters that replaced kings with strict and stern historical figures, like Cato or the Censor or the oppressive Brutus Queens were replaced with figures that symbolized virtue, like the strength of a soldier or prudence. Infantrymen became heroes.

The most well-known fortune-teller of the day Marie-Anne Adelaide lenormand used her studio to revolutionaries and nobles. This included Danton, Robespierre, Saint Just and all the intellectuals of the First Republic.

The same time there was a time when gypsies received a period that was a great deal of favor as future readers in different European courts as well as in the most elegant salons of the cities of the world. It was only natural that this would be the case at a moment when the fears, anxieties and uncertainty of life led to an unusual growth in divination and, more specifically the field of cartomancy.

In the latter half of the nineteenth century and early twentieth century the theories from Ephilas Levi, a prominent Esotericist from the past were developed in significant French and English religious fraternities.

Each society was able to have its own Tarot deck that outlined its esoteric principles.

In this way, adjusting themselves to the concept of the brotherhood of this or that The characters of the Tarot took on the most diverse designs that range from Egyptian, Kabbalistic, alchemical as well as astrological Masonic Neo-Templar and more. and up to the most recent variations.

Chapter 7: Discover The Major Arcana

Esoteric Significance

Major Arcana Major Arcana are really special cards that are unique and have no counterpart within the realm of cards.

When we look through the playing cards like the trumps and French fitting cards (poker cards) we see representations of "suits" that are very like the smaller arcana of tarot for instance, the major arcana also known as "Accomplishments" It is difficult to locate similar cards.

Particularly, the Accomplishments are 22 cards that are often with numbers ranging from 0 to 21 and each one bears an individual name, such as the one that symbolizes the magician.

In some decks, they can be used to address different names, such as for those of the Tarot de Marseille or Marseillais in which some characters like that of Pope as well as the magician can be replaced to using the Hierophant as well as the Bagatto or where the image representation is mirror in the Rider Waite decks.

Within the Tarot cards among them, the Arcana are the most dense in regard to esoteric symbolism.

They contain significant references to the importance in the arts of liberal learning (the instructors of the scholastic and initiatory classes of the middle age schools) as well as to hermeticism (an instigatory practice that is linked to mentors like Hermes) or many researchers have looked at the possibility of connections between Tarot and the astrological field, or maybe even worldwide of alchemy.

It also has a significant connection to Tarot cards and the Arcana as well as the realm of the Jews of Qabbalah as well as numerology. It is not uncommon that the Tarot cards are not only numbering with traditional numbers, but include the Hebrew letter, which symbolizes their connection to this kind of practice.

The Tree of Life, also known as the sephirotic trees, are the result of the synthesis of some of the most well-known and significant spiritual leaders in Kabbalah. Jewish Kabbalah.

It's a diagram that's abstract and symbolic, containing 10 elements, known as sefirot and arranged along three vertical pillars parallel to each other with three wings on the left 3 on the right, and four in the center The main pillar is over and beneath the two other pillars.

If one looks at the picture you can see the ten sefirot are linked with twenty-two channels. They are three vertical, seven horizontal and 12 diagonal.

Each channel corresponds to one of the twenty-two letters of Hebrew abjad. (sephirot).

Because of this powerful connection, the Tarot is often used for research into Qabbalah and numerology.

Information on Mystic Qabbalah

As I mentioned in the previous chapter, many esoteric specialists employ Kabbalistic interpretative techniques to finish the divinatory task.

In this chapter, I will provide the smallest details of some of the esoteric Kabbalah theories.

Be aware that these are extremely complex topics for those with a lot of experience, however I chose to include them to provide you with more food to think about and research.

In greater detail, I will explore the background of Kabbalah as well as the meanings of the numbers, as well as the connections.

13.1 What exactly is Qabbalah?

Kabbalah is a part of the esoteric heritage of Jewish mysticism, and specifically the spirituality that developed in Europe between the 7th and 8th centuries.

In Judaism the practice of receiving the tradition is known as qabbalah.

The foundation of Kabbalistic theory lies in The Hebrew Bible, or Tanach (an abbreviation for "Torah, Prophets, Writings").

According to Kabbalah the universe was formed from a primordial point via emanations, also known as sefirot. They are the same as numerations (sefirot) which are equivalent to divine names.

In its literal sense, sefirot refers to "calculation and number" and each represents an allusive representation of the Universe.

Each is an allegorical manifestation of the divine energy.

Sefirot sefirot are represented in a system called"the "Tree of Life" and are also connected with emotional and practical situations encountered by all of us throughout our lives, and comprise 10 fundamental concepts, which are evident in the chaotic and complicated variety of our lives and capable of uniting it , and giving its meaning and meaning.

The Tree of Life is an abstract symbol of symbolic meaning made up of 10 sefirot laid out on three pillars that are vertical:

Three on the left, 3 on the right as well as four more in the middle.

The central pillar is located above and below the two other pillars.

The Tree of Life diagram introduces an hierarchical and vertical division into four planes, or worlds that are states of conscious known as starting from the top Olam ha Atsiluth or World of Emanations, Olam ha Beriyah or World of Creation, Olam ha Yetsirah or World of Formations, and the final one, Olam as Asiyah, Olam ha Asiyah which is identified with the nature of man and the earth as objects created by God, which includes the determination of the physical as well as physiological law as the Sefirotic diagram that we are referring to is applicable to any manifestation, i.e., for both microcosms and macrocosms.

The four worlds could also be viewed as three because Beriyah (World of Creation) or Plane of Creation) and Yetsirah (World or Plane of Formations) can be seen as a single plane. Beriyah could correspond to what was traditionally referred to as "the Higher Waters, and Yetsirah could be a reference with the Lower Waters.

The first is associated as the Air element and are regarded as forming the sky's vault and the other with the Water element which is responsible for the rivers and oceans and oceans, which are joined by the horizontal line.

The former is associated by The former are identified with the Air element. They are regarded as the sky's vault The latter is associated are associated with The Water element, which forms the oceans and rivers, they are both joined by the horizontal line.

In them, all the inner and hermetic work gets done.

Six sefiroth are referred to by Kabbalah as the Kabbalah "of cosmic creation," correspond in the human being to the higher psychological state (Beriyah) as well as his lower mental state (Yetsirah).

The Tree of Life can also be divided into three columns with two visible side columns as well as an invisible central column, from which the two others project at a distance.

One of the two is positive, while and the other is neutral, and the third one is negative.

Through these foundations, the energy of creation continuously fluctuate and change.

The first is a reference to the division between planes in the same manner as columns or pillars; The second one includes an explanation of the Kabbalistic terms for each sefirah "numeration" and the alchemical and planetary relationships, since the planets have an intimate connection to their symbolic qualities of earth's metallic elements.

This cabalistic system is interspersed with the symbolic significance of numbers and the astrological meaning:

Zero Ain = Nothing The absence of.

1 Kether= Crown = first emanations of Being, without the astrological determinism.

2 Hokhmah = Wisdom: Fixed Stars.

3 Binah = Intelligence: Saturn.

4 . Hesed means Grace. Jupiter.

5 Gueburah = Penalty: Mars.

6 . Tifereth is Beauty. Sun.

7 Netsah = Victory: Venus.

8 Hod = Glory Mercury.

9 Yesod = The Foundation: Moon.

10. Malkhuth = Kingdom = Interaction between all four elemental elements. Earth.

13.2 Correlations with Qabbalah and Tarot

The meaning of symbolic numbers is crucial for those who want to discover the hidden meanings of cards.

1 Ace, which is the unity, is the primary that is always positive and helpful, symbolizing the beginning of the process of germination, or an affirmation for oneself. The four Aces of cards represent the Unity which is expressed in all four dimensions of Universal Being.

2. The number two is created through the unity that reflects its own polarization, creating an unidirectional law where two opposing and complementary principles exist in all forms.

The duality exists regardless of appearance, as opposites meet in a non-existent common point.

So above-below, forward-backward right-leftare concepts that always connect in a central point where the opposition vanishes.

It is , therefore, the symbol of the couple. It signifies a bond, however it is not a slack indicator of the danger that this includes: the conflict between two different ways to be, the battle and the competition.

3 The exchange of 1 and 2 creates the possibility of a new beginning point.

In three, we will be able to look at the quality of enlightening as well as constructive insight.

The number 3 is dynamic and is a reference to the actualization of something, that refers to the fusion of two numbers before, which are which are now joined by desire.

It is summarized in the geometric representation that is the triangular figure.

The four threes symbolize the energy of Saturn Also known as Kronos, Time; these four cards represent the four dimensions of time that could be depicted as dots as well as the spiral, circle and the straight line.

4. The four is the substance which is solidified, it provides stability, and may cause the sensation of pause or even immobility.

Four is connected to grace, and sums up the full potential of this instrument.

A symbol of development as well as stability and maturity, as a resemblance to the figure of the square which represents it, it is a reference to everything that is complete and solid but is limited in its rigidity.

4 . It is the primary manifestation number that regulates Creation's laws, direction of space, and the seasons of the year. It is linked to

Jupiter, the sun Jupiter and tin and energy that is positive and expansive "jovial" and friendly.

Five introduces a brand new element that "undermines the peace" of four. It causes it to be agitated. Five is linked to aggression, destructiveness, and even violence.

The symbol of renewal, unplanned and adventurous, and sometimes even marriage and success it was considered to be very good according to people of the Pythagorean school, but was questioned or even unlucky according to earlier customs.

Five, also known as the quintessence, or ether, is the center point where the four elements of creation meet which allows us to go back to the same.

It is connected to the warrior Mars who destroys the appearance of the material world and allows the universe to return to its fundamental source.

6 confrontation with the current reality Meditation, analysis and reflection.

When you have a number six, you are in into the world of beautiful connected to a number of decisions.

A sum made up of 2 opposing triangles symbolises the balance between two opposing polarities that are in constant contrast, and the attraction that is the reason for the inertia, the fight to be free from the limitations of love. Six is a number that represents harmony.

It also represents the symbol for alchemical gold, the ultimate state of all the metals, which represents the state of being created by the power of fire.

Seven is the outcome of the process that puts objects in motion.

The sevens have a connection to the sense of intuition creative love, travel, and intuition.

Similar to the fullness of the ancient system of planetary systems comprising the 7 planets and also with the seven notes of music and each week's seven days and the seven virtues, the seven sacraments, it represents intelligence, strength, harmony, movement.

Seven was believed as sacred by ancient people, distinctive, and immobilebecause it "does not exist and is unable to generate".

The I is the one that generates all of the following: two generates four and 8; the three generates the 6 and 9; and the 5 creates the 10, as seven is the sole one in denarius which generates zero, and which can be generated by the unity.

Is the sum of triad and the quadrilateral.

The many "scales" that it is able to give rise makes it a single and significant number.

8 The total of four plus four results in the octagon. It is the geometric shape that is the most similar to the circular. It refers to justice, and the fundamental stability that is the basis of, in their tempo the cyclic cosmic events that destroys and builds.

The interaction between male and female, night and day and the balance of opposing forces. It is the infinity cycle. A symbol for transformation. Realization.

Nine is perfect of the three. It is elevated to the level of power, symbolizing the protection of God, of the ideal of all that is distant from the world and the religious, as well as the spiritual quest. The number is a ritual and propitiatory one. Wisdom, understanding, expansion seeking satisfaction in the 10.

The number 10 represents the complete cycle in every aspect.

It symbolizes the Pythagorean Tetrakis, which is a symbol of spiritual awakening.

Unity, creation. A number that is split into 5 pairs to symbolize totality.

Chapter 8: Kabbalah Basics

The central idea behind Kabbalah is to return to the Garden of Eden' or, if you prefer, how to become part of the divine or increase your spirituality to the point that the frequency of your vibration in your soul begins to match the frequency of God.

According to kabbalists the first thing God designed is light. The nature of God is to provide light to the creatures of its creation and also to receive illumination from the creatures.

The term "light" is used to refer to conscious divine energy or soul, according to the kabbalists, before the light came, there was nothing, God forms the light and then creates darkness.

"And God created Adam in its own image, to be like God He created Adam: male and female God created them" Genesis 1:27

Kabbalists interpret this to mean because if God can be described as light then this must be the same for us.

This is the foundation of the concept of the trees of living. The illumination of the Divine is divided into 10 distinct expressions known as sefirot. Sefirot can be placed into the form of a tree. This tree is referred to as the tree of life, or the image of God.

The tree also symbolizes the soul's structure and when we become subconsciously aware of these sefirots you attain enlightenment. there is no need for drugs or any kind of material pleasure to feel happy. Neither do are we stressed, angry, or depressed in unfavourable circumstances, the impact of the environment or noise are minimal or not at all on our lives. Connecting directly to God, assist us get rid of unneeded desires and thoughts. By control of thoughts, feelings, and consciousness, our thoughts, emotions. We can take full control over our lives and our destiny.

Therefore, becoming part of the the tree of life is clearing your mind of negative thoughts and becoming fully conscious because now that you've become a part of the divine conscious and you aren't inferior to any other human being regardless of whether they are the president or president of America and Amazon CEO or A-list star.

Then Adam and Eve lived in the Garden of Eden happily, but then they decided to consume the forbidden fruit. As a result, they were removed from that tree. today they are forced to work long and hard in the earth to get food. Metaphorically, it signifies that we were overwhelmed by the negative energy and became caught in debt, gambling drugs, prostitution or revenge to escape this situation, it isn't an easy task until we are able to find light. that light could come provided in the form of assistance from a mentor, prayers and assistance from other souls, which could include your friends, relatives siblings, partners or even your parents or meditation, or a divine light can be capable of pulling you back. Another metaphor is that of the Israelites living in liberty in Israel but due to famine forced to go to Egypt and were slaves, and later were freed to regain their freedom thanks to the Moses' guidance. Moses.

Famine is an example of our mind being corrupted by an unexpected tragedy occurs in our lives, such as divorce, accident, or death of a partner or child similar to how Israelites were immediately enslaved in Egypt as well as our souls becomes instantly enslaved in despair, hopelessness, or a sudden loss of light and similarly to how Moses had the courage to grant Israelites free, we too have to discover the inner Moses to bring the inner light back and reconnect us to that tree which is the source of our life.

There is a reason for suffering in our lives, it destroys us entirely or helps us toward a higher level of consciousness, it is a way to be closer. Jews in Europe faced persecution but they realized that prosecutions could only end when they are more light-hearted than the rest, which is higher education, riches, and more information than the rest which is exactly what they did. this, so whenever we're going through a tough in the present, we need to recognize that suffering can only help to strengthen the light within us and that God is testing us to determine if we are able to become a part of the plant or not.

It is believed that the Kabbalists believe that the primary function of a creators is to provide light, similar to the sun's primary function is to generate energy. similarly, there comes the moment when creation also is a creator. Once the man has earned the amount of wealth he needs, they will become charitable, just as the sun can't hold energy and starts giving it away, similarly, wealthy people donates money or impart knowledge, since the value of giving is a part of the human spirit, and this method of giving is called "circuit".

Like everything else, it exists in pairs,'male-female darkness-light','matter-energy", "love-hate, wealth poverty, as the forces of good and evil and the good in us as well as the love of our God would like us to be the parts of the tree however, there's an evil component that takes us away from the light and hinders us from becoming part of the tree.

The good force of Judaism is called "Yetzer Hatov" is a reference to good will. However, the evil force is called "Yetzer Hara".

A man who is stuffed with food will never appreciate the flavor of food. For those who are in a constant state of hunger for the whole week even stale rice is as delicious as divine food that heaven offers someone who wanders in the scorching desert and the water of the oasis tastes better than wine that is the best, sun's first ray of light is only visible at the time of darkness as well, and similarly, the period before the sun's first light strikes the earth is the darkest and hence the time that passes before you are able to experience spiritual awakening is one of the toughest because there is a dark force that doesn't want to make you part of the tree, there will be doubts within your mind, which will leave you in a state of confusion However, should you succeed during that time, you'll gain entrance into the garden of Eden.

The Tree of Life in detail

To fully comprehend Kabbalah it is essential to comprehend that the life tree. that is the life tree. It, which has sefirots, which are ten parts.

The most popular representations of sefirots in the Tree of Life look similar to this: three sefirots left and three to the right and four on the middle. These three columns are called three pillars, which represent sefirot interplay and counterbalancing each other.

It is viewed as masculine while that left one is perceived as feminine. The masculine one is associated with giving, while the feminine pillars are linked to receiving, and the role of the middle pillars is to ensure the harmony between the two.

We could also suggest that the right and left pillars are very similar to Yin Yang. Yin is feminine , and is connected with receiving, whereas Yang is masculine and connected with giving. Furthermore, there is another mysterious energy by a yellow color that aids in the interplay between the two. For example, sperm that is male reproductive cells is masculine and has a smaller size. connects with ovary, a female reproductive cell and produces babies, and there is a an additional mysterious energy that helps both male and female cells to join together. This energy is known as god energy. It's like the third energy, which helps ovary and sperm to communicate, similarly, the middle pillar assists the right and left pillars to work together and to balance each other.

Another way to think about it is the human body. Our body is comprised of three major components, the first being our physical body which we can all see, which includes our hands, brain legs, legs, heart kidney, and the third is our memory, and cognitive abilities that could be described as a software part of us. The third component that keeps us alive or coordinated between our body components with software are our hearts that the mysterious energy.

In terms of computers, we could describe a computer system as consisting of three elements: the hardware that include CPU, monitor, keyboardand mouse, the software that can be windows and the last essential component to the interplay between software and hardware that is electricity. Without electricity, no computer system will function, and similarly, without soul the human being is unable to exist.

This idea is also known as trinity since without trinity, nothing could be created. In Christianity it is possible to define trinity means a combination of Divine Holy Spirit, Divine the Son.

Ten Sefirots

As we can see from the diagram, the 10 sefirots in the diagram are:

1) Keter- "Crown"

2) Chokhmah - "Wisdom"

3) Binah - "Understanding"

4.) Chesed = "Kindness"

5) Gevurah - "Discipline"

6) Tiferet - "Beauty"

7) Netzach - "Victory"

8) Hod - "Splendour"

9.) Yesod - "Foundation"

Ten) Malkuth - "Kingship"

Let's take a look at each one of the sefirots in depth.

Keter

The Divine Crown is the topmost of the sephirot it is situated found between Chokhmah as well as Binah (with Chokhmah on the right and Binah to the middle) and is situated over Tiferet. Keter can be described as the most obscure portion of Kabbalah It is beyond the human eye, as it is inaccessible and colorless. Keter's name is God connected to Keter is Ehyeh Asher Ehyeh (Hebrew: Ahyh Ashr Ahyh) The name by which God revealed who he was before Moses through the fire of the bush.

Hokhmah: Wisdom

Hokhmah signifies wisdom Hokhmah is the word for wisdom. If Keter is referred to as a first creative impulse which is the case, then Hokhmah is the first expression of it. It is the highest of the sephirots of the right line, since Keter symbolizes nothingness or the only mental structure, Hokhmah is the first consciousness-based intelligence that exists in Creation If you shut your eyes and stand still when a thought pops up to your mind. This thought is not from the beginning and is expressed as Hokhmah.

Hokhmah is blessed with two partszufim ("faces" also known as "features") which are the upper one is known as Abba Ila'ah ("the greater father") and the lower one is referred to in the form of Yisrael Saba ("Israel The Elder"). The two partzufim are collectively referred to by the name of Abba ("father").

Hokhmah is regarded as the primary source of inspiration in the creative process.

Binah: Understanding

Binah is the sephira number three. It lies beneath Keter just opposite Hokhmah It has four pathways, which lead to Keter, Hokhmah, Gevurah and Tif'eret. It is connected to the color black. Although Hokhmah is thought of as an idea flash, Binah is the actual advancement of thought.

Binah possesses two partzufim. The upper one is called Imma Ila'ah ("the higher mother") and the lower one is known as Tevunah ("comprehension"). Both of these are commonly referred to in the name of Imma ("the momma").

A thought that pops into your the mind is Hokhmah However, as we begin to think about this idea, it is connected to Binah in the midst of thinking about existing thoughts it is a time to be restricted by new ideas, and we can say Binah restrains Hokhmah. This is the reason the reason Binah is feminine while Hokhmah can be described as masculine. Binah and Hokhmah could be linked to reproduction. Hokhmah flowing with water. And just as the womb, which incubates a child, Binah develops thoughts.

Hesed: Mercy

Sefirah of creation is the term used to describe when we have shifted from the world of creation to the world of creation. This is called Yetzirah It includes the following sefirots.

The sefirots that are included in this group are Chesed Gevurah and Tiferet, Netzach, Hod and Yesod. Together, the six sefirot are referred to as the Microprosopus.

Each of these sefirots are connected to the attitude of qualities known as middot.

Hesed, which is on the right sides of the trees is the quality of kindness and is the right sides of a tree. It can be balanced with Gevurah which is one of the left. To enjoy unlimited kindness. It has to be restricted , and it is the responsibility of Gevurah.

The father's love or generosity to his child is never-ending but his unending love could destroy the future of a child at times, he may have to not accept the requests of the child or teach discipline to him, this action of love or restriction is accomplished by Gevurah.

In the Zohar Zohar, Hesed is associated with the patriarch Abraham due to the fact that Abraham has a love for God. God orders him to let go of all things and settle wherever God would like to set him. In another instance, he was willing to sacrifice his son in order to show his love for God.

Gevurah : Strength

Gevurah is believed to have the ability to limit the goodness of others prior to showering someone with unconditional love It is the responsibility of Gevurah to assess the love of a person. Gevurah can also be described to in Kabbalah in the form of "Midat Hadin" ("the attribute of judgement").

Together, Gevurah and Hesed remain in perfect balance. while the Chesed is working to draw other closer to us, Gevurah is able to choose between deterring those who are deemed unworthy or to sever the person who is in love with them.

Gevurah is thought to be one of the forces which created the universe. it is responsible for the withdraw of the divine, known as 'Tzimtzum when the withdrawal is completed. it creates the ground for chess to take place in the process of creation.

Sometimes we feel compelled to do something make us want to take action like trying gambling or using drugs. Gevurah provides us with the courage to resist these urges.

So Gevurah grants us the desire to be separated from the love.

Another instance of Gevurah could be the government making a decision to either withdraw or reduce subsidy. A subsidy is a benefit the government gives to its citizens, however, at when it comes to achieving a better good, the government will have to stop providing the subsidy. the withdrawal or reduction of subsidy could put citizens in temporary pain and we all know that for the good of the long run, this pain is required.

In Abrahamic religions, we practice fasting. It has a important meaning, we consider food and water for given, which is why we do not feel love or affection for them. But if we continue to fast or stay away from water and food and are hungry for a long period of time and then our affection for the food returns, and Hesed as well as Gevurah are neither adversaries nor complementary.

Tiferet Beauty Balance, Beauty, Integration

Tiferet is the integration with Hesed and Gevurah. Hence its location is in the middle. Tiferet is linked to the third patriarch Jacob and is which is also called Israel.

Tiferet symbolizes the persona of God His hands are mercy, and the left is Gevurah.

Tiferet helps to maintain the equilibrium in Hesed and Gevurah One force is expansive while the other forces are restrictive Without

Tiferet one force can easily dominate the other and could cause destruction, which is the goal of Tiferet to keep them in balance.

Tiferet also is able to balance Netzach as well as Hod in the same way. In that scenario, Hod is thought of as the intellect whereas Netzach is viewed as emotion.

Tiferet is connected to all the other sephirot, with the exception of Malkuth.

NETZAKH: Eternity

Netzach is regarded as the seventh sefirot. It is situated below Hesed and is a reference to perpetuality, victory or endurance. Netzach is located geometrically in the middle of Hod. The biblical name of Netzakh refers to Moses, Moses is a person who by his perseverance helped children of Israel towards freedom.

If Moses not persevered and remained persistent, he would not have received orders given by God. Divine, Netzakh is known as perseverance, which is required for obtaining the illumination from God.

If we're trying to attain spiritual awakening or illumination sometimes we can feel discouraged or even deviated if we failed to persevere, which is often referred to as Netzach. Netzach has also been associated with the leadership since as the light within us grows, we are capable of influencing others around us. This is the reason God chose Moses to share the message of his Netzakh.

HOD: Glory

The eighth sephira is part of the Kabbalistic Tree of Life. It is comprised of four paths that can lead into Gevurah, Tiphereth, Netzach and Yesod.

Hod is also linked to humility and gratitude. HOD is the opposite of Netzakh in the same way that Netzach is connected with leadership qualities, HOD is of followers and sometimes being a follower can be good.

When you travel the path of becoming Kabbalists You may meet others Kabbalists who have more experience and more wisdom than you. So when they share their wisdom, you must to be humble and grateful and abide by their instructions, similar to in the classroom. Your professor could have dedicated an entire life to this topic, and in order to absorb his wisdom, you must to be humble.

This means that Hod is in opposition to Netzakh You can be a an effective leader only if you're a good follower first. To create more light within you You must be humble and open to those with more light than you.

Yesod: Foundation

Yesod is regarded as the organ of reproduction, whose seeds are the generative energy of all creation.

Sperm are regarded as the cells that are the birthplace of life, it takes the efforts of various body parts as well as hormones and our minds which all work together to create sperm. Once the sperm are produced and then released, it's the responsibility of the penis to move them into a male body part that causes the birth of a human being. The divine makes this process enjoyable, and once the sperms are released, an orgasm can be felt and is the sensation of pure joy.

Yesod is therefore the component of a tree, which gathers vital energy of the sephirot higher and transmits these vital and creative energy into that feminine Malkuth below. Therefore, Yesod is thought of as the channel that transmits the light Malkuth receives.

Yesod is thus viewed as a medium by which the creator forms an emotional connection to the creator.

The creation journey is the most joyful that is humans create babies. It is possibly the reason the creator created creation to feel the joy of the creation.

MALKHUT: Kingdom

Malkhut is the 10th sephirot. It is located in the middle of the tree, just below Yesod the tenth of sephirot. This sephirot bears an image for the wedding.

Malkhut symbolizes Shekhinah according to certain Kabbalists, it's the union of God and Malchut that creates harmony in the world.

The kabbalists can experience this by bringing our awareness (kudsha Brikh hu) to the content of our awareness(shekhinah).

The Zohar compares malchut with the moon that has no illumination of its own. However malchut is the ultimate manifestation to the Divine Light, the source from which all the process began. it was in the spirit of malchut that all sefirot were released. Therefore, malchut is also the receiver and the finalization of giving.

How do you do it? Kabbalah

To experience the divine light and become a Kabbalist is what seekers of spirituality have been doing for centuries.

The amount of time needed to become a Kabbalist is dependent on your spiritual level.

Understanding and reading Zohar, Zohar is considered as the Holy Grail of Kabbalism The more you understand Zohar the more God will show you the light of its rays.

Meditation on sefirot by meditating upon the 10 sefirot symbols is crucial for me, I have a huge picture of sefirot in my prayer room in which I meditate prior to sunrise for an hour. the most important thing is to comprehend the meaning behind the ten sefirot when I meditate. typically, I sit and meditate by listening to gregorian theological chants.

Begin by focusing on the first sefirot Kether and contemplate for two minutes about what it represents. Kether is a symbol of God, which is undiscovered, as you focus upon this image for 2 minutes, you can move to the next, Hokhmah which signifies wisdom continue to focus upon this sign for 2 minutes, and then you can move to the next symbol Binah which is the symbol for understanding. Now, focus on the next symbol Hesed which is a symbol of love and Mercy. After two minutes of concentration on Hesed you can move on to the next symbol

Gevurah that signifies withdraw or 'strength'. Move to Tiferet this time, which symbolizes the balance between withdraw and love in the meantime, move to the next symbol Netzakh that symbolizes perseverance followed by HOD which is a symbol of humility, after that the final symbol is Yesod and finally Malkhut The process can take approximately twenty minutes.

Continue this practice of meditation in accordance with the your own light. Within a few weeks, you'll begin seeing a greater amount of illumination in yourself as well as your progress towards awakening.

Fasting is also a crucial element during the mystic journey for those who are new, one week of fasting is enough. If one week of fasting is difficult, go for a single fast each month in which you are completely removed from water and food during a minimum of 12 hours. it aids in strengthening the Tiphareth and to keep the balance between the sefirots.

Avoid slander and insignificant gossips. When we make a fuss, we are wasting time dispersing negative energy around us as well as in the surroundings Refraining from these actions can bring us closer to the light.

Be around people who radiate positive energy and possess more light as light is the source of light and darkness creates darkness. Certain people emit negative energy through the use of words, vibes and actions, so mingling with them will dim the light inside you and push you more distant from the Divine.

Three ways to awaken spiritually is to practice the the threefold path of prayer, meditation and charity.

Aspects of Kabbalah

When it comes to the principles of Kabbalah are in question, there are fundamental theological differences in Judaism as well as Kabbalah. Keep in mind that there are certain distinct similarities between both, so if you find yourself looking at things that are similar to yours there's an obvious reason behind that. But it's essential to note that there was an obvious and apparent gap between the two religions and you'll surely be amazed at the things that make Kabbalah distinctive. So, without further delay, let's explore what is what makes Kabbalah an intriguing complex, multifaceted and controversial religion in the world.

God Heard and Hidden:

Kabbalah affirms the existence of two sides of God that must be reconciled with us and we can comprehend. Ein Sof the one they refer to God is an entity that is infinite in its transcendence, and is unlimited as well as inaccessible. The truth is that the divine cannot be understood by us and the divine being would be beyond our understanding when we try to comprehend the motives and facts that God intended for us. This is referred to as the hidden God and it places us in a serious disadvantage as humans who are in serving God. We can't possibly comprehend, or predict the things God does, how God does it or how we can participate in God's plan of action.

But, there's another option other side of the coin that you may find it helpful in understanding. There is the manifestation of God that is revealed to us all through this persona we think of as God. To comprehend and understand the things that God desires through the universe which is all around us. The way God interacts with us is another way we can see and comprehend the Revealed God However, this is the only way through which acts that we begin to understand what God the Revealed God is seeking to accomplish. But, we should also be aware the fact that this Revealed God represents the image that God wants us to perceive and it is important to recognize that this aspect of God communicates a lot about God's intentions and motives in addition.

www.ingramcontent.com/pod-product-compliance
Lightning Source LLC
Chambersburg PA
CBHW050404120526
44590CB00015B/1826